T0065757

PREVIOUSLY BY JAY LUVAAS:

Frederick the Great on the Art of War

Napoleon on the Art of War

Selected, Edited, and Translated by

Jay Luvaas

A TOUCHSTONE BOOK
PUBLISHED BY SIMON & SCHUSTER
NEW YORK LONDON TORONTO SYDNEY SINGAPORE

TOUCHSTONE
Rockefeller Center
1230 Avenue of the Americas
New York, NY 10020

First Touchstone Edition 2001
TOUCHSTONE and colophon are trademarks of Simon & Schuster, Inc.
Designed by Kim Llewellyn
Manufactured in the United States of America
3 5 7 9 10 8 6 4

The Library of Congress has cataloged the Free Press edition as follows:
Napoleon I, Emperor of the French, 1769–1821.
[Selections. English. 1999]
Napoleon on the art of war / selected, edited, and translated by
Jay Luvaas.
p. cm.
Includes bibliographical references and index.
1. Napoloeon I, Emperor of the French, 1769–1821—Military
leadership Sources. 2. Military art and science—France—
History—19th century Sources. 3. Napoleonic Wars, 1800–1815—
Campaigns Sources. 4. France—History, Military—19th century
Sources. I. Luvaas, Jay. II. Title.
DC214.L88 1999 99-13248
355.02—dc21 CIP

ISBN 0-684-87271-4
ISBN-13: 978-0-684-87271-1

To my daughter, Karen

Contents

INTRODUCTION

This book has been in the making, off and on, since 1966, when my *Frederick the Great on the Art of War* was published. Had anyone suggested then that it would be three decades before Napoleon finally emerged, I probably would never have started this project.

The basic research was done in the first twenty years and perhaps six chapters were more or less complete when I left Allegheny College in 1982 for Carlisle, Pennsylvania, where I served as visiting professor of the U.S. Military History Institute at Carlisle Barracks. I set the book aside for that year intending to pick it up later, but then was invited to move across the street to the U.S. Army War College to become their first Professor of Military History.

Here I immediately became immersed in the effort to keep up with my students—colonels and lieutenant colonels on the fast track and an occasional general officer—and to publish materials relevant to their interests and needs. There was no time for my own work during the week. I could never find those long, unbroken periods that I needed to spend with Napoleon. Indeed, not until retiring from the War College two years ago did I have the time—and the energy—to return to the book.

My decade-long hiatus from Napoleon was probably a blessing in disguise, for my students at the War College had raised many issues that gave me new insights and questions to ask of Napoleon. Moreover, until the U.S. army rediscovered the operational art in the mid-1980s (see Chapter 10), I had not been aware of Napoleon's mastery of this intermediate level of war. A strong case could be made that Napoleon created the operational level of war as it is understood and practiced by soldiers today. Without the corps—which Napoleon organized and manipulated so skillfully—it would have been impossible for commanders to function effectively at the operational level.

But, behind the military genius was a man who often overreached himself. After World War I, Field Marshal Foch wrote what may have been Napoleon's most fitting epitaph: "He forgot that a man cannot be God; that above the individual is the nation, and above mankind the moral law: he forgot that war is not the highest aim, for peace is above war."

Napoleon on the Art of War

I

Creating the Fighting Force

Napoleon's genius for war lay not so much in the domain of tactics or even of strategy as in administration, organization, attention to details, and his capacity for work. In the words of F. M. Kircheisen, a Napoleonic scholar, "his principal military triumphs since 1800 must be ascribed not so much to the measures taken shortly before or during the course of fighting, as to his amazing talent for organization, and his perfect arrangements for the march." No one in his day better understood that an army was "an aggregation of details," a "chain of innumberable links."

In Germany each village has its lord who designates recruits for the army without consideration for either their rights or conveniences. In France the army has always been recruited by means of the lot, which was known under Louis XIV, Louis XV, and Louis XVI as "calling out the militia," and currently as conscription. The privileged classes were exempt from drawing for the militia; nobody was exempt from being conscripted. In effect this was the militia without privilege, which made it as disagreeable for the privileged classes as the militia had been for the masses.

1. Conscription was the most equitable, easiest, and most advantageous method for the people. Its laws have been so perfected under the empire that there is no need to change anything, not even the name, for fear this might lead to changes in principle. Those departments which since 1814 have been separated from France have asked for and been granted, as a benefit, the continuation of the conscription laws in order to avoid the arbitrary, unjust, and annoying Austrian or Prussian laws on recruitment. The Illyrian Provinces, long accustomed to Austrian methods of recruitment, have never ceased to admire French conscription laws, and since returning to their former empire they have been allowed to continue under the French system.

2. During the first decade of the Revolution the armies were recruited by requisition, which involved all citizens from eighteen to twenty-five years of age. There was no drawing by lots or serving by substitute. Conscription laws applied only to young men upon reaching the age of twenty; they were obligated to serve only five years, which provided the advantage of training a large number of soldiers who would be able to defend the country in moments of crisis. It would be appropriate to extend the length of service to ten years—in other words to the age of thirty-five years in the active army and five in the reserves. It is from age twenty-five to fifty that man is in his prime, therefore it is the most favorable age for waging war.[1]

We need men and not boys. No one is braver than our young people, but lacking fortitude they fill the hospitals and even at the slightest uncertainty they show the character of their age.[2] It is urgent that we get rid of all soldiers unfit for service and who must be fed and supplied without being useful.[3] Eighteen-year-old boys are too young to wage war . . . far from home. . . . Being too young, none should be sent to the field army. Instead, they should remain in France, where they will be clothed, armed, and drilled.[4] I think that even defaulting conscripts, men twenty-two, twenty-three, and twenty-four years of age, would be better than the others. Mixed with our soldiers they would take a liking to the service.[5]

We must encourage soldiers by every method to remain with the colors: this will be accomplished by demonstrating great regard for the veteran soldiers and honoring them in three classes, and by giving five sous to the second, and ten sous to the first. It is a great injustice not to pay a veteran more than a recruit.[6]

France has a population of 40,000.[7] One million souls provide from 7,000 to 8,000 conscripts a year; nearly . . . half this number is necessary to meet the needs of the government, the Church, and of the arts. An annual draft of 3,500 men would provide 30,000 over a ten-year period, making allowances for death; 15,000, men would constitute the army of the line, another 15,000, the army of reserve. Of the former, 6,000 would be kept under arms for twelve months, 4,000 others for three months, and an additional 5,000 for fifteen days—that would be equivalent to 7,000 men for the entire army. . . . The 15,000 men of the army of reserve would not be taken from their jobs or their homes except in case of war.[8]

The military institutions of the English are faulty. They recruit only for money, although they often empty their prisons into their regiments. Their discipline is cruel. Given the education and the kind of soldiers they have, they can get only mediocre noncommissioned officers from the ranks, which forces them to increase the number of officers beyond all proportion. Each battalion drags hundreds of women and children in its retinue; no other army has so much baggage. Officer commissions are for sale; lieutenancies, companies, and battalions are purchased. An officer may be at the same time a major in the army and a captain in his regiment, a bizarre practice most prejudicial to all military esprit.[9]

Military discipline admits of no modification.[10] The army must understand that discipline, wisdom, and the respect for property support its victories, that pillage and theft belong only to the cowardly, who are unworthy of remaining in the ranks . . . that they plot the loss of their honor and that they have no goal other than to stain the laurels acquired by so much bravery and perseverance.[11] Without discipline there is no victory.[12]

I recommend that you take pleasure in reading your muster rolls. The good condition of my armies stems from the fact that I devote an hour or two each day, and when the muster rolls of my troops and my fleets, comprising twenty large volumes, are sent to me each month, I set aside every other task to read them in detail and to note any changes in them from one month to the next. I get more pleasure from this kind of reading than a young girl gets from reading a novel.[13] I advise you to devote one hour every morning to reading your muster rolls in order to know the position of all the units in your army.[14]

Napoleon to Marshal Berthier, Chief of Staff, 9 March 1805

I beg you to have made for me an account of the army's state of affairs.

The first column will contain the regiments by armies and by military divisions.

The second column, the number of men that were present under arms at the most recent review. . . .

The third column, the number of men in hospitals or on furlough, and included among the effectives.

The fourth, the number of men provided by conscription this year.

The fifth, the number of men assigned to the regiments from levees called up from the reserves for the last two years.

The sixth, the number of men that would be needed to place all battalions on a full peace footing and to complete the corps forming the three camps of Saint-Omer, Bruges, and Montreuil, of 2,400 men.

The seventh, the number of men detached to the colonies. You will reveal if these detachments are made by pickets or by companies, and if the latter you will name the battalion. If it is by picket, give the number of officers.[15]

Napoleon to General Berthier, 25 March 1803

Order the different division commanders to unite all detachments from their respective regiments during the months of April through September. When the situation permits, the entire regiment of all cavalry squadrons will be united, and in the small fortified towns there will be at least one battalion or two squadrons. . . . You will exempt from this order those detachments of scouts that have been sent along the frontiers to prevent smuggling.

Recommend to division commanders that they see to it that the troops work at instruction and that there is uniformity in the evolutions, that the conscripts are issued uniforms—or at least jackets—immediately, and that in the fall maneuvers they are all trained in the *School of the Battalion* and can perform the firing drill as early as this year.

Recommend as well that regiments that are within reach of water train their horses to cross rivers, that all dragoon regiments perform dismounted drill, even when they have no muskets, and that you issue one musket to every fifty men to begin their first instruction.

As for the artillery, I think that the first inspector will have given the necessary instructions so that the duty for that is followed with the greatest activity. My intention is that in each regiment of mounted artillery notice will be taken of those gunners sighting the piece who hit the most targets, that you take similar note of the men working with mortars and howitzers who have lobbed the most shells into the [target] circle, and those who will have fired the most shells.

From September 2nd to the 7th each of these regiments will send its ten best gunners to La Fère, where they will be trained in large artillery drills consisting of firing siege guns, field artillery on their carriages, howitzer and mortar batteries, hot shot, and every other kind of fire, in order to determine which of these eight regiments will supply the best man who aims a gun.[16]

Napoleon to General Marmont, commander of the camp at Utrecht, 12 March 1804

Familiarize yourself with the details of large infantry maneuvers. The weather will soon permit you to begin drilling the troops, and you know the full importance of that, especially in war, where the first moments are apt to be the most lively and decisive. You must set the tone for the officers so that all are occupied with training. . . .

Take good care of the soldier and look after him in detail. The first time that you arrive at camp, draw up the troops facing each other by battalions and inspect the soldiers, one by one, for the next eight hours. Listen to their complaints, inspect their arms, and satisfy yourself that they do not lack anything.

There are many advantages in making these reviews last from seven to eight hours. It accustoms the soldier to remain under arms; it demonstrates that the commander takes his responsibilities seriously and devotes himself completely to the soldier, which in turn inspires the soldier's confidence. Leave them of course with the belief . . . that I will come to see them maneuver and present them with their colors.[17]

I strongly recommend that you have the troops maneuver as much in small groups as in the school of the battalion, so that they are accustomed to deploy rapidly while those who come in ranks perform fire by files.[18] Recommend to your division commanders that they make their troops go through the firing drill twice a week, that they have target practice twice a week, and finally, that they perform the drill evolutions three times a week. Have them form columns of attack by battalion, charge in column of attack, and deploy under the covering fire of the first division, with everyone firing upon reaching a line of battle.[19]

Similarly, you will form the column of attack while the center division opens fire by file and deploys under the fire by file. After that, have them execute in advance of 100 paces the drums beating *Advance* with a simple and steady beat, and have each platoon perform the fire by file as it arrives to take its place in the line of battle. You will also order that they often practice the maneuver of quickly forming into a battalion square by forming into columns behind the rear divisions of the battalion at platoon intervals and firing by file. This is the maneuver that is most necessary for colonels to master, for the least hesitation could compromise the regiment.

Finally, direct that each *voltigeur* company be instructed in promptly forming the square and immediately opening fire by files, so that as skirmishers sent out in front of the battalion they can quickly reunite and fight off cavalry. Issue the necessary powder for these exercises and announce that these maneuvers are most especially what I will have performed in my presence.[20]

Napoleon to Marshal Marmont, commanding VI Corps of the Grande Armée, 17 April 1813

Of all the maneuvers I must recommend to you the most important, which is to form squares by battalions. The battalion commanders and the captains must know how to perform this movement with the greatest speed, for it is the only way to protect themselves against cavalry charges and to save the entire regiment. Since I assume that these officers are little skilled as tacticians, acquaint them with the theory and explain it to them every day so that this maneuver becomes second nature to them.[21]

Three fourths of the people . . . have no idea at all of the differences among troops.[22] You would do well to remember that [at the battle of Bailén in 1808] General Dupont's army was composed of recruits, and that this affair, although excessively poorly handled, would not have happened to veteran troops, who would have had enough esprit to offset the mistakes of the general.[23]

I value the bravery, fidelity, and loyalty of the Swiss, and this feeling has induced me to decide that all Swiss regiments should consist of Swiss citizens without any mixture of deserters or other foreigners.[24] Russian troops are brave, but far less so than the French: the experience of their generals and the ignorance and sluggishness of their soldiers make their armies actually less formidable.[25] The Poles are the French of the north: they are a brave people.[26] Russian troops are inferior; the Germans more so, and the Italian troops are more inferior still, and yet the Italians have been in the ranks for a dozen years and are intermingled with many French soldiers, and have spent four years at the camp of Boulogne.

My system would be in great jeopardy were I to regard the Westphalians as reliable soldiers. Of all the allied troops they are the ones that I most mistrust. It is therefore not large numbers of troops that you must apply yourself to have, but a small number of good troops that you can train progressively.[27] Nor do I approve of the organization of colonial battalions. This notion of putting arms in the hands of wretched subjects is a fatal one.[28] Moreover, refractory conscripts should never be assigned to the artillery, sappers, or cavalry.[29]

An army composed of men from different nations will not hesitate to commit foolish mistakes. . . . The military art would be to expect these mistakes and to benefit from them.[30] Greeks in the service of Alexander the Great felt no passion for his cause. The Swiss in the service of France, Spain, and of some Italian princes had no passion for their cause. Frederick the Great's troops, composed in large measure of foreigners, had no passion for his cause.

A good general, good cadres, good organization, good instruction, and good discipline can produce good troops, regardless of the cause they fight for. It is true, however, that fanaticism, love of country, and national glory can better inspire young soldiers.[31]

II

Preparations for War

"The real objective of having an army is to provide for war," noted former U.S. Secretary of War Elihu Root, but "preparation is based on organization . . . and means far more than the mere organization of the army and navy." Some of Napoleon's keenest observations concern preparation for war. He believed that secrecy, discipline, and morale were key to his many successes in the field.

Wartime is not the same as peacetime. In war every delay is fatal. Manifestly you need order, but this order must be of a different kind than in times of peace. During peace, war consists in furnishing nothing except through the required red tape; in time of war it consists in granting as much as possible without any formality except for the returns that help keep things accurate. A regiment might have 300 dismounted men in its depot and only twelve or fifteen horses. One has to make inquiries, but start first off by giving it 300 horses, 300 saddles, and 300 bridles, so that this regiment provides me with 300 effectives in the presence of the enemy.

Because I must follow peacetime procedures all of my work is unduly slow. The economy today causes it. One dismounted conscript at one cavalry depot is a waste to me and is of no use. . . . But let me impress upon you the importance . . . of the damage that could result from a false sense of economy or inappropriate rigidity. There is always time later to put things in order.[1]

Simply gathering men together does not produce soldiers: drill, instruction, and skill are what makes real soldiers.[2] But soldiers and units amount to nothing if they are not well drilled. Make them perform maneuvers; have them take target practice; look after their health.[3]

I cannot repeat it too often: act with prudence, do not compromise poor troops, and never be so foolish as to believe, like so many people, that one man automatically equates to one soldier. Troops of this nature among your soldiers require the most redoubts, earthworks, and artillery. Such soldiers need the four guns per battalion as prescribed in the regulations. . . . Inferior troops need a larger proportion of guns.[4] There are some corps that request only a third of the artillery needed by other corps.[5]

Discipline

The success of an army and its well-being depend essentially upon order and discipline, which will make us loved by the people who come to greet us and with whom we share enemies.[6] Pillaging destroys everything, even the army that practices it. The inhabitants leave, which has the dual drawback of turning them into irreconcilable enemies who take revenge upon the isolated solider, and of swelling the enemy ranks in proportion to the damage that we do. This deprives us of all intelligence, so necessary for waging war, and of every means of subsistence. Peasants who come to peddle provisions are put off by the troops who stop them, pillage their wares, and beat them.[7] When I arrived [in Italy in 1796] the army was injured by the bad influence of the troublemakers: it lacked bread, discipline, and subordination. I made some examples, devoted all of our means to reviving the administrative services of the army, and victory did the rest. . . . Without bread the soldier tends to an excess of violence that makes one blush for being a man.[8]

We will never forget to make a disciplinary example of these soldiers who deviate from the rule of severe discipline.[9]

INTELLIGENCE

I must have precise information to adjust my movement and formulate my plan.[10] I need to have very detailed information, to know the width and length of islands, the elevations of mountains, the width of canals . . . the nature of fortified cities, fortress by fortress, [and] the condition of roads. . . . All of this interests me in the highest degree.[11]

The barbarous custom of having men beaten who are suspected of having important secrets to reveal must be abolished. It has always been recognized that this way of interrogating men, by putting them to torture, produces nothing worthwhile. The poor wretches say anything that comes into their mind and what they think the interrogator wishes to know.[12] Study the country: local knowledge is precious knowledge that sooner or later you will encounter again.[13]

In war, spies and inquiries count for nothing: that would be to risk the lives of men on very poor estimates that cannot be trusted.[14]

Instructions for General Bertrand, 25 August 1805

General Bertrand will go directly to Munich . . . after which he will proceed to Passau. There he will inspect the condition of this fortress, go back up the Inn as far as Kufstein, where he will make a proper reconnaissance—the situation of the positions, their distance, the condition of roads, the width of the river, the amount of water, the alternating domination of one or the other of the banks, the ferryboats, the bridges, and the fords. He will be accompanied by some Bavarian engineers but he will take care to see everything for himself and he will write what the engineers could tell him about the conditions on the river and events that have occurred there.

Next he will follow the Salza as far as Salzburg; from there he will return to Munich by crossing the Inn at Wasserburg, and again write a memorandum of this third reconnaissance. He will gather all the information at Munich from very knowledgeable sources on the defiles of the Isar and other rivers that flow in the Tyrol as far as the defile of Lech.

From Munich he will go to Füssen without leaving Bavarian territory. If Füssen is not occupied by the Austrians he will examine it in detail.

From Füssen he will descend the Lech and make a complete reconnaissance as far as the Danube. He will reconnoiter Ingolstadt and Donauwoerth along the Danube and, in going from one to the other, he will have seen the Danube at Passau and he will make notes every time that he sees it from Donauwoerth.

He will make a reconnaissance of the Regnitz as far as Mein; and he will return from Bamberg to Ulm by the route that he will judge appropriate. From Ulm he will go to Stuttgart, always by small stages and traveling only during the day. From Stuttgart he will proceed to Rastadt and make a good reconnaissance of the road from Ulm to Rastadt from the military perspective and that of the general staff. In all these trips he will make a point to trace carefully the road from Ulm to Donauwoerth along the left bank of the Danube; from there to Ingolstadt, and thence to Ratisbon, then on to Passau in search for information. While at Passau he will reconnoiter the road leading into Bohemia as far as possible in Bavarian territory and get information on the rest. Could one travel to Prague by this route?

He will make detailed reconnaissance on the small stream of Ilz, and the nature of the roads and the terrain from the source of the Ilz that descends the mountains into Bohemia as far as the mouth of that river. What is the width of the valley, the nature of the roads, the main cities, and the ease or disadvantages that an army would have moving along the right bank of the Danube, and by this means turning the Inn and moving on Freystadt with an eye toward moving into Moravia.

Gather all information on the fortifications that the enemy might have constructed at Linz, or Steyer, or any other place as far as—and including—Vienna.

From Rastadt he will return to Fribourg, thence to Donaueschingen and from there to Basle; and from there he will come and rejoin me at Huningue, without entering Swiss territory; along the right bank of the Rhine he will make a reconnaissance of the position of Stockach.

M. Bertrand will write from Strasbourg to acquaint me with all the rumors in the country about war, peace, and Austrian movements. He will go to Stuttgart, where he will see M. Didelot [the French plenipotentiary] . . . to discuss the Austrian forces in the Tyrol. . . .

Everywhere his language will be pacific. He will speak of the expedition against England as being imminent, with the troops embarked. He will display no anxiety, even to our own agents. He will pay no attention to Austrian preparations: they could not begin the war—that would make no sense.[15]

Napoleon to Prince Eugene, 30 September 1805

If you have the time, make a reconnaissance of Lake Majeur as far as the foot of Simplon, to determine if it can be crossed and also to have an accurate picture of it in your own mind. After that make one to the foot of Saint-Gothard. At your age [twenty-four] such reconnaissances are made quickly and they remain in your mind for life. . . . Have someone of intelligence in the Valteline inform you of enemy movements.[16]

Napoleon to Marshal Berthier, 3 March 1806

Enclosed you will find a decree naming M. de Lagrange, captain in the 9th Dragoon Regiment, second secretary to the legation in Vienna. Summon him and make sure he understands that I intend him to keep an accurate statement of the strength of the Austrian regiments and their locations, and that for this purpose he should have in his cabinet a chest divided by compartments, in which he will place cards containing the names of the generals, the regiments, and the garrisons, and that he will change the compartments following any movements that they undertake. Each month he will send you the returns of these movements, adding to it the changes that the regiments could experience in their organization.

This mission is very important. It is essential that M. de Lagrange keep complete records and not misplace a single Austrian battalion.[17]

Napoleon to General Bertrand, 4 March 1807

Your letter tells me nothing. You will however have to be able to interrogate in order to know the names of the regiments and the commanding general and a hundred things, all very important—the morale of the troops, the way in which they are fed, the strength of the different units, and what is known from conversations with the colonels and officers of the corps.

I expected several pages and I get only two lines. Redeem all that by writing me in great detail.[18]

Observations on Affairs in Spain, 27 August 1808

It is always asserted that we do not have intelligence, as if this situation were extraordinary in an army and it was a routine matter to find spies. In Spain, like everywhere else, we must send detachments sometimes to seize either the curé, or the acolyte, occasionally the head of a convent or the postmaster, and especially to confiscate all letters and sometimes even to seize the mail carrier. Place them under arrest until they talk, by having them interrogated twice a day. Hold them as hostages and charge them with giving information to the enemy.

When you know how to take forceful and energetic measures, you will get information. You must intercept all the mail. . . .

Beyond doubt, even within French lines, the inhabitants are all informed about what is going on and this would be much more the case beyond our lines. Who therefore can object if we take prominent men, retain them for a while, and then release them without doing them any harm. It is . . . a fact that when one is not in a desert but in an inhabited country and the general is not informed, it is because he does not know how to take the necessary measures to get information. The services that inhabitants render to the enemy general are never for affection, nor even for money. The most that they have to gain is the protection of their property, village, or monastery.[19]

MAPS

It is very important . . . to have good maps of all the country between the Adige, the Po, and the Adda . . . which will probably be the theater of new wars on the same scale as the large map of Italy.[20] It is necessary to have all reconnaissances made at the Topographical Bureau of War in order that we could, if necessary, send the generals all suitable instructions. Then, from the commencement of war, they would know the defensive campaign fieldworks that will have to be prepared in the various positions in case of unfortunate developments.[21]

I believe that the topographical engineers work, but I am not sure that they work according to good fundamental principles. We have them produce registers of the survey of lands and not military maps, which means that in twenty years we shall have nothing. I have had occasion to be convinced of this in the departments of the Rhine, where I was presented with large maps that were almost useless. We had invested four years, and I don't know how many engineers and how much money, to map only a portion of the department of the Roër, and we have nothing for the departments of Rhine and Moselle and Mont-Tonnerre, which are truly important. To take twenty years to finish maps and plans is to work too much for posterity. . . .

How many circumstances could occur over the next twenty years that we would regret? If one of them had been on the scale of a Cassini map[22] we could already have had all of the Rhine frontier. How many circumstances could occur over the next twenty years where we will regret them? . . . What events can occur, even for this accumulation of paper, before we can reap any advantage from all this work? I don't know why war is waged with this type of map. . . . The fact is, I have not had, on my visit to the Rhine, any map where I could gain any knowledge of the country. We have to draw maps of Mont-Blanc, the Piedmont, the Italian Republic, the Ligurian Republic, and the Papal Estates. There is no lack of work, therefore, for the geographical engineers. But if we follow for Mont-Blanc . . . and the Piedmont the same progress that we followed for the departments of the Rhine, nothing will be finished in our lifetime.

Engineers are too much masters of what they wish to do. I have not asked for anything other than the completion of the Cassini map. Rest assured that the operations are not directed on projects that are too vast. Experience proves that the greatest defect in general administration is to want to do too much: that results in not having what is needed. . . . Order them especially to mark clearly the nature of the different roads, in order to distinguish those which are practicable or impracticable for artillery. If all the debouches of the

Black Mountains are accurately located, this map will be one of the most essential that we could have.[23]

Napoleon to General Clarke, 19 December 1809

I order that the map of Germany, which has been made at the *Dépôt de la Guerre,* be sent back. It is so bad that I cannot use it. I would rather have the first map captured in a library. This mixture of good and bad portions is fatal—worse than if all the parts were bad—for it serves only to jeopardize important operations. I know of nothing more dangerous.

When it comes to maps, we must have only good ones, or else the dubious or poor sections must be colored to indicate that one should not trust them. Moreover, I am not pleased with the map that you presented me for the four departments of the Rhine. I want it to be on the scale of that of Cassini . . . and you propose a map on a scale one-eighth smaller. . . . The Depot of War is poorly managed. . . . [24]

When I ask for a reconnaissance I do not want someone to give me a plan of campaign. The word *enemy* must not be used by the engineer! He must reconnoiter the roads, their condition, the slopes, the heights, the gorges, and the obstacles, and verify if the vehicles could cross there, and completely forgo any plans of campaign. . . . Two or three engineers will be assigned to each of these reconnaissances: they will study the country thoroughly. Two or three engineers will be charged with each of these reconnaissances.

When the army marches, the geographical engineers, who will have reconnoitered the country, will always be at headquarters in order to provide all necessary information. Their reconnaissance memoranda should always be written in the simplest style and be purely descriptive. They should never stray from their objective by introducing extraneous ideas. An accurate method is the only one that pleases the Emperor.

They will give the length, width, and quality of the roads; they will accurately sketch the detours of the roads, which often are explained only by bizarre features of terrain. The rivers must also be carefully traced and measured . . . their bridges and fords marked. The number of houses and inhabitants of the towns and villages will be indicated. Insofar as possible they should measure the heights of the hills and mountains, so that one can easily determine the dominant points—these heights need be only relative to each other. You cannot go into too minute details on this and many other points, but you must always convey, in the simplest manner, how the thing is depicted in the eye of the observer.

There will be a consistent scale for all the maps.[25]

SECRECY

See to it that no information concerning the military frontiers of the empire is published that you have not permitted, and that you will deny permission for anything that could provide the enemy with useful information.[26] The minister of general police will notify all journalists that they cannot be permitted to print anything in their papers pertaining to the movements of ground and sea forces.[27] Prohibit gazettes along the border . . . from mentioning the army, as if it no longer exists.[28]

DECEPTION

Napoleon to General Clarke, 10 October 1809

I desire that you write the King of Spain [Joseph] to make him understand that there is nothing more contrary to military principles than to make known the strength of his army, whether in Orders of the Day and proclamations or in the gazettes. Tell him that when he is induced to reveal the strength of his forces he should exaggerate and present them as formidable by doubling or trebling the number, and that when he mentions the enemy he should diminish his force by half or one third.

In war everything is mental, and the King strayed from this principle when he stated that he had only 40,000 men and proclaimed that the insurgents have 120,000. This discourages the French troops by representing enemy numbers as immense, and gives the enemy a poor opinion of the French by proclaiming his weakness throughout

Spain. In brief, it gives moral strength to his enemies and takes it away from himself. Man is naturally inclined to believe that in the long run numbers must be defeated by greater numbers.

On the day of battle the best-trained soldiers have difficulty in evaluating the number of men in the enemy army, and in general it is a natural instinct to be inclined to see the enemy as being larger in numbers than he actually is. But when one has the imprudence to allow . . . exaggerated estimates of enemy strength . . . every cavalry colonel on reconnaissance sees an army, and each light infantry captain sees whole battalions. . . .

In war, intellect and judgment are the better part of reality. The art of the Great Captains has always been to . . . make their own forces appear to be very large to the enemy and to make the enemy view themselves as being very inferior. . . .

The soldier cannot judge, but the intelligent officer, whose judgment is fairly good and who has knowledge of affairs, pays little attention to the Orders of the Day and to proclamations and knows how to evaluate events. . . .

When I defeated the Austrian army at Eckmühl, I was outnumbered five to one, and yet my soldiers believed that they were at least equal in strength to the enemy. Even today, despite the long time that has elapsed since we were in Germany, the enemy does not know our real strength. We make a point of making our numbers appear larger every day. Far from admitting that I had only 100,000 at Wagram, I continue to pretend that I had 220,000 men.

And constantly in my Italian campaigns, where I had a handful of everything, I exaggerated my strength. That served my plans and did not diminish my glory. My generals and the trained soldiers know well—after the event—how to recognize all of the capacity of operations, even that of having exaggerated the numbers of my troops.

With trifling considerations, small vanities, and petty passions, it is never possible to accomplish anything great.[29]

In Egypt I had agreed with all of the colonels that, in the Orders of the Day, we would inflate by one third the real quantity of the total distribution of provisions, arms, and clothing. Thus the author of the *Military Précis of the Campaign of 1789* was astonished to learn that the Orders of the Day for this army had shown its strength to be 40,000, when other authentic information that he had received gave its effective strength as far less. In the reports of the Italian campaigns of 1796 and 1797, and since, the same means have been used to give exaggerated ideas of French strengths.[30]

In 1800 . . . as soon as we had news of the commencement of hostilities in Italy and the direction that enemy operations were taking, I considered it necessary to march directly to the assistance of the Army of Italy. But I preferred to debouch by the Great Saint-Bernard Pass in order to fall on the rear of Melas's army, seize his magazines, his parks, and his hospitals, and finally to give battle after having cut his communications with Austria. The loss of a single battle was to cause the total loss of the Austrian army and make possible the conquest of all Italy. To execute such a plan required speed, profound secrecy, and great audacity. The secret was the most difficult kind to keep, for how is it possible to conceal their movement from numerous English and Austrian spies?

The most suitable way . . . was to reveal it myself by making such a demonstration that it would become an object of ridicule to the enemy, and to act in such a way that the enemy considered all of these declarations as a way to create a diverson to the operations of the Austrian army, which blocked Genoa. It was necessary to give a specific objective to the observers and spies.

Therefore it was decided in messages to the Legislative Corps, the Senate, and by decrees and publication in the papers, and finally by insinuation of every kind, that the place where the army of the reserve would assemble was Dijon, that I would review it there, etc. Immediately all the spies and observers gravitated to this city. They saw there, during the first days of April, a large officer establishment without an army, and in the course of this month, some 5,000 or 6,000 conscripts and retired soldiers, many of them disabled and moved by their zeal rather than their physical strength.

Soon this army became an object of ridicule, and when I held the review on 6 May, people were astonished to see only 7,000 or 8,000 men, most of them not even in uniform. . . . These misleading reports circulated through Brittany, Geneva, Basle, London, Vienna, and Italy. Europe was filled with caricatures, one of them representing a child twelve years of age and an old invalid with a wooden leg, with the caption that read "Bonaparte's Army of Reserve."

However, the real army was formed en route. The divisions were organized at different points of rendezvous. These places were isolated and had no connection with each other. . . . The most difficult thing to conceal was the movement of needed provisions through arid mountains where nothing could be found. We forwarded 100,000 rations to Toulon to be sent to Genoa, but 1,800,000 rations were directed to Geneva, put aboard ship on the lake, and unloaded at Villeneuve when the army arrived there.

At the same time that the formation of the army of reserve was announced with the greatest ostentation, a number of small bulletins were prepared which, in the midst of many scandalous anecdotes about myself, it was demonstrated that the army of reserve did not and could not exist, that at the most we could unite some 12,000 conscripts. . . .

The combination of all of these means of putting the spies on the wrong scent was crowded with the most fortunate success. It was said in Paris, as in Dijon and Vienna: "There is no army of the reserve." At Melas's headquarters it was added, "The army of reserve, which threatens us so much, is a band of 7,000 or 8,000 conscripts or invalids, with which they hope to deceive us into abandoning the siege of Genoa. The French count too much on our naïveté; they would have us read like the fabled dog who leaves his prey for a mere shadow."[31]

III

A Military Education

According to Frederick the Great, "War is not an affair of chance. A great deal of knowledge, study, and meditation is necessary to conduct it well." Napoleon devoted much thought to military education. He stressed applied mathematics, the drill evolutions, map reading, field maneuvers, and a study of the Great Captains—Alexander, Hannibal, Caesar, Gustavus, and Frederick the Great—men who, in Major General J. F. C. Fuller's words, exhibited "imagination operating through reason, reason operating through audacity, and audacity operating through rapidity of movement."

Napoleon to General Clarke, Minister of War, 1 October 1809

Our soldiers are not very well instructed. You must occupy yourself with two works, one for the school at Metz and the other for Saint-Cyr.

The text for the school at Metz must contain the ordonnances on fortified cities, the decisions that have disgraced all commanders who have thoughtlessly surrendered a fortified city entrusted to their defense, and, finally, all ordonnances of Louis XIV and of our own day that prohibit surrendering a fortified city until a breach has been made and the passage of the ditch is practicable. In this work, which will comprise several volumes, it is necessary to include a dissertation on the defense of fortifications that would make the reader appreciate—

1. How real soldiers, upon assuming command of a fortress that had been nearly dismantled, could in a short time put it into condition to withstand a long siege. You must go into great detail in this respect and cite fifteen examples, such as that of the Duc de Guise at Metz and the Chevalier Bayard at Mézières.

2. How these brave commandants, anticipating the attack of the enemy, immediately repaired the breach and intrenched the bastion; and also how the smallest work and a good defense of the worst works have considerably delayed the progress of the besiegers. You could cite the last siege of Danzig, where a simple blockhouse made us devote fifteen days to crowning the covered way and the passage of the ditch.

In this context it is necessary to protest against this mania that induces engineer officers to believe that a fortress can be defended only for a given number of days. Make them understand why this is absurd and cite known examples of sieges where, instead of the number of days that had been calculated for advancing the parallels, the besiegers had been forced to spend a much longer time at it because of sorties from the fort, crossfires, or some other kind of delay that the defenders of the fortress had created. Make them understand that when a breach is made, all of your resources still remain, provided the counterscarp is not destroyed and all artillery fire is not extinguished, and how even the assault on the breach can fail if you have intrenched behind it.

I include here only a survey of the ideas that are necessary in this work: it is a substantial project to execute and I believe that [Lazare] Carnot or some other man of his stature would be most appropriate to be placed in charge. The objective must be to make it understood how important is the defense of fortified cities, and to arouse the enthusiasm of young soldiers by a large number of examples: to make known how, in every situation . . . the rules of siegecraft had been constantly delayed in their application.

And finally, in this work you should include a large number of heroic deeds by which the commandants who have defended the most mediocre fortifications for a long time are immortalized, and recall at the same time the judgments which, in all nations, have dishonored those who had failed to fulfill their duty.

Only the author can conceive how this work should be divided; I have given only a general sense. He must treat not only that which pertains to the engineer officer, but also the commandant and the governor of a fortress. He must study a few cases where it was necessary to spread false rumors that the enemy could propagate and state in principle that a commandant of a besieged fortress should consider all ways of thinking relevant to his mission, that he must regard himself as being isolated from everything; and finally that he must have no other idea than to defend his fortress . . . until the last minute, conforming to what is prescribed in the ordonnances of Louis XIV and the example of brave men.

I attach great importance to this work, and he who performs it will be well rewarded. It must be at one and the same time a work of science and of history. The narrative sometimes must even be entertaining. It should stimulate interest, contain details, and if necessary have plans added to it. But it must not, however, be over the heads of . . . the young men.

As for the work for the military school, I desire that you cover the administration on campaign and the rules of encamping so that each knows how to lay out a camp, and finally the duties of a colonel or a commander of an infantry column. It is especially necessary to stress the duties of the officer who commands a detached column, in order to clearly convey the notion that he must never give up all hope, that if surrounded he must not surrender; that in the open country there is only one way for brave men to surrender, and that is—like Francis I and King John—in the midst of the melee and under the butt end of muskets; that to capitulate is to try to save everything with honor, but that, when one emulates Francis I, at least he can say, as Francis did, "All is lost except honor!"

You must cite examples such as that of Marshal Mortier at Krems, and a great number of others that fill our annals, to demonstrate that in the past armed columns have found a way to break out by seeking all of their resources in their courage, that he who prefers death to ignominy saves himself and lives with honor, while on the contrary the man who prefers life dies by covering himself with shame.

Thus one can select in ancient or modern histories all deeds committed to excite admiration or contempt. Among the shameful actions be sure to include the affairs of Blenheim and Höchstaedt, and that of the body of French Grenadiers who, in the Seven Years' War, surrendered. One can even cite the affair of General Dupont, who, as relief columns were advancing, decided that he was defeated in the first attack and preferred, in order to save the baggage, to obtain a phony capitulation which was not fulfilled and thus also dragged down the other divisions in his loss.

There are a large number of historical examples, for and against, that you must select and cite so as always to inspire admiration for the one and contempt for the other.[1]

The Art of War

Tactics, the evolutions, the science of the engineer and of the artillerist can be learned in treatises, much like geometry, but the knowledge of the higher parts of war is acquired only through the study of history of the wars and battles of the Great Captains, and from experience. There are no precise or fixed rules. Everything depends upon the character that nature has bestowed upon the general, on his qualities and faults, on the character of troops, on the range of arms, on the season, and on a thousand circumstances that are never the same.[2]

Education, strictly speaking, has several objectives: one needs to learn how to speak and write correctly, which is generally called grammar and belles lettres. Each lyceum has provided for this object, and there is no well-educated man who has not learned his rhetoric.

After the need to speak and write correctly comes the ability to count and measure. The lyceums have provided this with classes in mathematics embracing arithmetical and mechanical knowledge in their different branches.

The elements of several other fields come next: chronology, geography, and the rudiments of history are also a part of the education of the lyceum. . . . A young man who leaves the lyceum at sixteen years of age therefore knows not only the mechanics of his language and the classical authors, the divisions of discourse, the different figures of eloquence, the means of employing them either to calm or to arouse passions, in short, everything that one learns in a course on belles lettres. He also would know the principal epochs of history, the basic geographical divisions, and how to compute and measure. He has some general idea of the most striking natural phenomena and the principles of equilibrium and movement both with regard to solids and fluids.

Whether he desires to follow the career of the barrister, that of the sword, or English, or letters; if he is destined to enter into the body of scholars, to be a geographer, engineer, or land surveyor—in all these cases he has received a general education necessary to become equipped to receive the remainder of instruction that his circumstances require, and it is at this moment, when he must make his choice of a profession, that the special studies present themselves.

If he wishes to devote himself to the military art, engineering, or artillery, he enters a special school of mathematics; the *polytechnique.* What he learns there is only the corollary of what he has learned in elementary mathematics, but the knowledge acquired in these studies must be developed and applied before he enters the different branches of abstract mathematics. No longer is it a question simply of education, as in the lyceum: now it becomes a matter of acquiring a science. . . .

History

History can, by analogous considerations, be compared to the sciences for which it would be useful to have a special school. The way to read history is in itself a real science. Everything has been said and repeated. The apocryphal historians multiply, there is such a vast difference between one book and another on the same subject written in different epochs . . . that he who would seek sound knowledge and is suddenly placed in a vast historical library finds himself thrown into a veritable labyrinth.

To know what remains from the ancient historians and all that we have lost, to distinguish the original fragments of supplements written by good or bad commentators, is in itself almost a science, or at least an important object of studies. Thus the knowledge and the selection of good historians, good memoirs, and genuine chronicles of the time is a useful and genuine knowledge. If, in a great capital such as Paris, there were a special school of history and the student initially would take a course in bibliography a young man, instead of spending months wandering around in inadequate or unreliable readings, would be directed to the best works and would more easily and quickly attain better instruction.

Moreover, there is a part of history that cannot be learned from books—modern history. No historian gets up to our own times. For a man twenty-five years of age there is always a gap of fifty years preceding his birth for which there is no history. This gap leads to many difficulties, requires a work that is always imperfect and often useless, in order to make one's way from past events to the present. This would be an important function of the professors of the special school of history. They must know not only what has happened since the foundation of empires until the epoch where historians have taken over, but even up to the present moment.

There must be many professors. It would be necessary to have one each for Roman history, Greek history, the history of the late Roman Empire, ecclesiastical history, the history of America, and several others for the history of France, England, Germany, Italy, and Spain.

History would be divided . . . by subject matter. . . . The history of legislation would be given top priority. The professor would have to go back as far as the Romans and move forward to modern times by covering successively the different reigns of the kings of France up to the Consulate.

Next should come the history of French military art. The professor would elucidate the different plans of campaign adopted in various periods of our history, either for offensive war or for defending our frontiers, the reason for success or the cause of failure, the authors and memoirs where one could find details of the events and evidence of the results. This part of history, which interests everybody and is so important for soldiers, would be of the greatest use for statesmen. At the special engineering school one would show the art of attacking and defending fortified cities. The art of war cannot be depicted on a large scale because it has not yet been created, if indeed it ever can be. But a chair of history where one could elucidate how our frontiers have been defended by the Great Captains in the different wars would produce very great advantages. . . .

Something is lacking in a great state where the young studious male has no way of receiving good direction in what he wishes to study and is forced to grope his way and waste months and years of searching through useless readings for the real meat of instruction. . . . I desire these institutions: for a long time they have been the object of my thoughts because, having worked a great deal, I personally know how much they are needed. I have studied much history and often, for lack of a guide, have been forced to lose considerable time in useless readings. . . . I have devoted enough interest to geography to know that there is not a single man to be found in Paris who is perfectly informed of the discoveries that occur each year and the changes that happen incessantly.

I am persuaded that the establishment of such a school would be of great use for general instruction, even for men who have received the most advanced education. The course of literature would have none of these advantages because—according to my own experience—it teaches nothing beyond what a person knows at age fourteen. . . .

My hidden agenda is to assemble all men who follow, not philosophical history or religious history, but the history of actual events . . . up to the present. All our young men find it easier to learn about the Punic Wars than the war of the American Revolution, which ended in 1783. . . .

It matters little that the historian is more or less removed from the events, provided he deals with them accurately. Indeed, he will be all the more truthful because his readers, being contemporaries, can all be judges. . . .

Without this establishment . . . it would be a long time before soldiers possessed the means of learning how to benefit from mistakes that have caused reverses, or to appreciate the dispositions that could have prevented them. The entire war of the French Revolution could be fertile in lessons, and to learn them it is often necessary to work long, in vain, and in extensive research. The problem is not that the detailed facts have not been written . . . but that nobody has bothered to make the research easy and to give the necessary direction to make it with discernment.[3]

True truths . . . are very difficult to obtain in history. . . . There are so many truths. Fouché's "truth," for example, and other intriguers of his ilk. Even the "truth" of many honest men will occasionally differ from my truth. All too often historical truth, so much implored and which everyone is eager to invoke, is only a word. It cannot exist even at the time it happens, in the heat of conflicting passions. And if, years later, there remains agreement it is only because the interests and the adversaries are no longer with us.

So what, then, is this "historical truth" most of the time? A fable agreed upon, as it has been very aptly stated [by Voltaire]. In all these matters there are two essential portions that are very distinct—material facts and moral intentions. The material facts would seem to be bound to be indisputable, yet see if any two accounts agree. There are disputes that remain in eternal litigation. As for moral intentions, how can these be recovered even assuming good faith on the part of the writer? And what will it be if they are motivated by bad faith, special interest, or passion?

I issue an order, but who can read the depth of my thought or my real intention? And how each is going to catch hold of this order, measure it according to his own standards, and bend it to his plan or his individual system. . . . Yet this is history. I have seen people dispute me over my own thoughts of a battle, the intent of my orders, and decide against me. . . . It makes no difference: my adversary or opponent will have his partisans.

This is what has persuaded me not to write my private memoirs, to introduce my own feelings from whence naturally sprang the nuances of my private character. I cannot stoop to confessions like Jean-Jacques [Rousseau]. . . .

Often great depth and subtlety will be attributed to what was perhaps the simplest alternative. People will credit me with plans that I never made. For a long time they will argue about knowing if my absolute authority and arbitrary acts stemmed from my character or my calculations; if they were produced by my inclination or by force of circumstances; if my constant wars came from my inclination, or if I was driven only to do it reluctantly; if my immense ambition, which is so much reproached, acted as a guide or the eagerness of domination or the thirst for glory, the need for order, or the love of general comfort, for it deserves to be considered under these different faces.

It is known that I did not insist on bending circumstances to my ideas, but that, as a general rule, I let myself be influenced by them. But who can, in advance, respond to fortuitous circumstances or unexpected events? How many times, therefore, have I been forced to completely change [my plan]. Also I have acted from general principles far more than from resolved plans. . . .

There is probably no person who, according to his own way of perceiving things, does not attribute to my real system the fantastic result of his own calculations, and from that again comes the fable agreed upon that will be called history. It could not be otherwise.

My greatest deeds have been attributed to luck, and people will not fail to charge my reverses to my shortcomings, but if I were to write of my campaigns people would indeed be astonished to see that in both instances my judgment and abilities were always exercised only in conformity with principles.[4]

THE GREAT CAPTAINS

All of these Great Captains of Antiquity . . . and those who, much later, have deservedly marched in their footsteps, have performed great deeds only by conforming to the rules and the natural principles of the art of war—in other words, by the precision of the combinations and the intelligent relationship between ends and means, and of efforts with obstacles. They have succeeded only by conforming to the principles, whatever the boldness of their enterprises and the extent of their success. They have not ceased to make war into a veritable science. For this reason alone they provide our great models, and only by emulating them should we hope to approach them.[5]

No great actions are the product of chance and luck: they must always proceed from calculation and genius. Rarely does one see the great men fail in their most perilous enterprises. Consider Alexander, Caesar, Hannibal, Gustavus Adolphus, and other Great Captains. They always succeeded. Is it because they were lucky that they thus became great men? No! But being great men, they knew how to master chance. When one desires to study the sources of their success, he is quite astonished to see that they have done everything to obtain it.

Alexander the Great

Alexander, when scarcely more than a small boy and with a mere handful of troops, conquered one fourth of the globe, but was this on his part a simple eruption or an unexpected deluge? No. Everything is profoundly calculated, executed with audacity, and conducted with wisdom.[6]

Alexander waged eight campaigns, during which he conquered Asia and a part of India. . . . In 334 B.C. he crossed the Dardanelles with an army of nearly 40,000 men, one eighth of them cavalry. He stormed across the Granicus in front of the army of Memnon, a Greek who commanded on the coast of Asia for Darius, and spent the entire year of 333 B.C. establishing his power in Asia Minor. . . . In 332 B.C. he encountered Darius, who, at the head of 600,000 men, was in position near Tarsus . . . defeated him, entered Syria, seized Damascus . . . and besieged Tyre. This superb center of the world's commerce delayed him for nine months. He captured Gaza after a siege of two months, crossed the desert in seven days, entered Pelusium, then Memphis, and founded Alexandria. . . . In less than two years, after two battles and four or five sieges, the coast of the Black Sea from Phasis to Byzantium, that of the Mediterranean as far as Asia Minor, Syria, and Egypt, had succumbed to his arms.

In 331 B.C. Alexander recrossed the desert, encamped at Tyre, traversed the Syrian depression, entered Damascus, crossed the Euphrates and the Tigris, and on the fields of Arbela defeated Darius, who in this battle had a much larger army than he had led at Issus. Babylonia opened its gates to him. In 330 B.C. he took . . . Susa, Persepolis, and Pasargadae. . . . In 329 B.C. he went back toward the north . . . [and] extended his conquests as far as the Caspian Sea. . . . In 328 B.C. he captured by force the rock of Oxus, received 16,000 recruits from Macedonia, and subdued the neighboring peoples. . . . In 327 B.C. he crossed the Indus, defeated Porus drawn up in battle array . . . and planned to cross the Ganges, but his army refused to do it. . . . In 324 B.C. he marched again toward the north, crossed at Ecbatana, and ended his career at Babylonia, where he died of poison.

His war was methodical and is worthy of the greatest praise. None of his convoys was ever intercepted, his armies always progressed by growing stronger. They were weakest at Granicus, in the beginning. On the Indus they had tripled, not counting the troops under the orders of the governors of conquered provinces, which were composed of sick and exhausted Macedonians, recruits sent from Greece or formed by Greeks in the service of the satrap, or levied among the natives. . . .

Alexander deserved the glory that he has enjoyed over the centuries and among all peoples, but suppose he had been defeated at Issus, where the army of Darius was in battle array along his line of retreat, with his left anchored on the mountains and the right at the sea . . . or at Arbela, having the Tigris, Euphrates, and the deserts in his rear, without fortified depots, 900 leagues from Macedonia, or by Porus and driven into the Indus.[7]

What I love about Alexander . . . is not the campaigns themselves . . . but his political means. He left behind, at age thirty-three, an immense, well-established empire that the generals divided amongst themselves. He had the art of making conquered people love him.[8] He showed himself to be at one and the same time a great warrior, politician, and lawgiver. Unfortunately, when he attained the zenith of his glory and success, either his head turned him or his heart was spoiled.[9]

Hannibal

In 218 B.C. Hannibal left Carthage, crossed the Ebro, the Pyrenees—which were unknown up to that time to the Carthaginian armies—crossed the Rhone, the coastal Alps, and in his first campaign established himself in the midst of the Cisalpine Gauls, who were always the enemies—and sometimes the conquerors—of the Roman people. . . .

It took him five months to make this march of 400 leagues. He left no garrison or depot in the rear, nor did he preserve his communication with Spain or Carthage until after the battle of Trasimene. No more vast or extended plan has been executed by man. Alexander's expedition was not nearly so bold and was much easier: he had many more chances of success. It was wiser!

Nontheless Hannibal's offensive war was methodical: the Cisalpines of Milan and Bologna became Carthaginians for his purposes. Had he left fortresses and depots in his rear he would have weakened his army and compromised the success of his operations. He would have been vulnerable everywhere.

In 217 B.C. Hannibal crossed the Apennines, defeated the Roman army on the fields of Trasimene, converged around Rome, and moved on to the lower coasts of the Adriatic, where he communicated with Carthage for the first time.

The following year, 80,000 Romans attacked him: he defeated them at Cannes. Had he marched six days later he would have been in Rome and Carthage would have been mistress of the world. Nonetheless, the effect of this great victory was immense. Capua opened its gates and all the Greek colonies and a large number of cities in southern Italy followed fortune and abandoned the cause of Rome.

Hannibal's principle was to keep his troops united, to have a garrison only in one captured fortress which he preserved in good condition in order to keep his hostages, large machines, distinguished prisoners, and his sick, leaving his communications the responsibility of his allies. He maintained himself in Italy for fifteen years without receiving any help from Carthage and evacuated it only by the orders of his government to fly to the defense of his own country. Fortune betrayed him at Zama and Carthage ceased to exist. But had he been defeated at the Trebbia, at Trasimene, or at Cannes, what worse things could have happened to him? Defeated at the gates of the capital, he could not keep his army from entire destruction. And had he left half of his army or even a third at the first and second bases, could he have been victorious at the Trebbia, at Cannes, or at Trasimene? No! All would have been lost, even his armies in reserve. History would know nothing about him.[10]

Caesar

Caesar was forty-one years of age when he commanded his first campaign in 58 B.C. . . . Three hundred thousand Helvetians had left their country to establish themselves on the ocean coasts; they had 90,000 armed men and invaded Burgundy. The people of Autun appealed to Caesar for help.

Caesar left Vienna, a fortress in the Roman province, moved up the Rhone, crossed the Saône at Châlon, reached the Helvetian army a day's march from Autun and defeated it in a long-contested battle. After forcing the Helvetians to return to their mountains he recrossed the Saône, seized Besançon, and marched through the Jura to fight the army of Ariovistus, which he encountered and defeated several marches from the Rhine, forcing it to return into Germany. . . .

In this campaign he constantly kept the six legions that comprised his army united in a single camp, leaving his allies to look after his communications. He always had a month's supply in his camp and several months of provisions in a fortress where, following Hannibal's example, he kept his hostages, magazines, and hospitals. He followed these same principles in his seven other Gallic campaigns. . . .

In his Civil War campaigns Caesar triumphed by following the same methods and principles, but he ran far greater risks. He crossed the Rubicon with only a single legion, seized thirty cohorts at Corfinium, and drove Pompey from Italy in three months. What swiftness! What suddenness! What audacity! And while he prepared the necessary boats for crossing the Adriatic and following his rival in Greece, he crossed the Alps and the Pyrenees, marched through Catalonia at the head of 900 horsemen, which was scarcely sufficient for his escort, and arrived in front of Lérida, in the camp of his lieutenant . . . and in forty days he subdued Pompey's legions commanded by Africanus, crossed the distance separating the Ebro from the Sierra Morena like a thunderbolt, pacified Andalusia, and returned to make his triumphant entry at Marseilles, which his troops had just captured. Finally he reached Rome, where he was dictator for ten years. . . .

In 48 B.C. Caesar crossed the Adriatic with 25,000 men, held all of Pompey's forces in check for several months, and then, rejoined by Antony, who had crossed the sea in the midst of Pompey's fleets, he marched united on Dyrrachium and invested his opponent's fortified depot. . . . Not content with having invested this city, Caesar next proceeded to invest the enemy's camp. He took advantage of the summits of the surrounding hills, occupied them with twenty-four forts that he had built, and thus established a line of contravallation six leagues in length. Pompey, driven back to the sea, received provisions and reinforcements from his navy, which dominated the Adriatic. Taking advantage of his central position, he attacked and defeated Caesar, who lost thirty colors and several thousand soldiers, the elite of his veterans.

Caesar's fortune seemed to falter. He could not hope for any further reinforcements. The sea was denied him, and all advantages were on Pompey's side. Caesar made a march of fifty leagues, carried the war into Thrace, and defeated Pompey's army at Pharsalus. . . . Nearly alone, although master of the sea, Pompey fled to the coast of Egypt, where he was killed at the hands of a base assassin. Several weeks later Caesar arrived on his trail, entered Alexandria . . . [and] finally, after nine months of constant dangers and combats, the loss of any one of which could have meant his ruin, he triumphed over the Egyptians. . . .

Caesar's principles were the same as those of Alexander and Hannibal: keep the forces concentrated, do not be vulnerable at any point, move swiftly against important points, taking into account psychological conditions, the reputation of one's arms and the fear that they inspire, and also taking the political means to keep allies loyal and conquered peoples obedient, to give every possible chance to assure victory on the battlefield and to concentrate all of one's troops there.[11] He was at one and the same time a man of great genius and great audacity.[12]

Gustavus Adolphus

Gustavus Adolphus crossed the Baltic, seized the Pomeranian island of Rügen, and carried his arms over the Vistula, the Rhine, and the Danube. He fought two battles. Victorious on the field at Leipzig, he also won the battle of Lützen, where he was killed.

Such a short military career has bequeathed great memories—his great boldness, rapid movements, order, and the intrepidness of the troops. He was animated by the same principles that guided Alexander, Hannibal, and Caesar. . . . [13] In eighteen months he won one battle, lost another, and was killed in the third. His reputation was certainly acquired cheaply. . . . Tilly and Wallenstein were better generals. No masterly movement on his part is recorded; he abandoned Bavaria because of the maneuvers of Tilly, who understood how to force him to evacuate the country, and he let Magdeburg fall before his very eyes. That's a neat reputation for you![14]

Turenne

Turenne is the greatest French general of all. . . . His last campaigns are superb. His great merit is not to have committed any mistakes.[15] Turenne waged five campaigns before the Treaty of Westphalia, eight between that treaty and the Treaty of the Pyrenees [1648–59], and five after that until his death in 1675. His maneuvers and marches during the campaigns of 1646, 1648, 1672, and 1673 were conducted along the same principles as those of Alexander, Hannibal, Caesar, and Gustavus Adolphus.

In 1646 he left Mayence, descended the left bank of the Rhine as far as Wesel, where he crossed the river, moved up the right bank to the Lahn, united his force with the Swedish army, crossed the Danube and the Lech, and thus made a march of 200 leagues to traverse enemy country. Upon reaching the Lech he united all of his troops under his own hand, having, like Caesar and Hannibal, left his communications to his allies, or rather he consented to separate himself momentarily from his reserves and communications while reserving a fortified depot for himself.

In 1648 he crossed the Rhine at Oppenheim, joined the Swedish army at Hanau, moved on the Regnitz, fell back to the Danube, which he crossed at Lauingen, fought a battle with Montecuccoli, whom he defeated at Zusmarshausen, then crossed the Lech at Rain and the Isar at Freysing. The Bavarian court abandoned Munich in dismay. Turenne next moved his headquarters to Mühldorf, where he levied a contribution, and ravaged the entire electorate to punish the Elector for his bad faith.

In 1672, under the orders of Louis XIV, Turenne directed the conquest of Holland. Descending the left bank of the Rhine as far as the point where this river divides into several channels, he crossed the Rhine and seized about sixty fortified towns. His advance guard extended as far as Naarden. We do not know what prompted him to stop and not enter Amsterdam. The Dutch, when they recovered from their surprise, opened the floodgates and inundated the country. Weakened by the garrisons that it had stationed in the captured fortresses, the French army did nothing more. The King returned to Versailles, leaving Marshal de Luxembourg in command.

Turenne crossed the Rhine with a detached body of troops to march to the relief of the army of the bishops of Münster and Cologne, the King's allies. Moving up the right bank he got as far as the Main, where he held in check the 40,000 men of the Great Elector until the moment when this prince, having been joined by the army of the Duke of Lorraine, was forced to cover himself by the Rhine, which permitted the enemy to move against Strasbourg, where the Prince de Condé arrived in time to destroy the bridge and once again cause the plan of the Great Elector to fail. The latter then marched upon Mayence and threw up a bridge within artillery range of this fortress, flooding the right bank with his detachments. During the winter Turenne recrossed to the right bank using the bridge at Wesel, defeated the Great Elector, drove him against the

Elbe and on 10 April forced him to sign his separate peace with France.

Such bold and long marches struck France with astonishment, and until they could be justified by success they were the object of criticism by mediocre men. Had Turenne built bases every thirty leagues and left armies in reserve, they would have been defeated in detail.[16]

I am all the more impressed by Turenne in his operations because he acts exactly as I would have done in his place. He passed through all the grades, having been a soldier for one year, a captain for four, etc. He is a man who, had he come near me at Wagram, would have immediately understood the situation. The same would apply to Condé as well, but not to Caesar or Hannibal. Had I such a man as Turenne to assist me in my campaigns, I would have been master of the world. . . . Condé was a natural-born general, Turenne a general by experience. I consider him much better than Frederick [the Great] of Prussia. In Frederick's place he would have accomplished much more and he would not have committed the King's mistakes. Turenne's genius would have been just as superior for conducting grand armies as well as small ones.[17]

Frederick the Great

Frederick the Great was much bolder than I.[18] The battle of Leuthen is a masterpiece of movements, maneuvers, and resolution. It alone would suffice to immortalize Frederick and place him in the rank of the greatest generals. He attacked an army stronger than his own, in position and victorious, with an army composed in part of troops which had just come from being defeated, and he gained a complete victory without paying casualties disproportionate to the result.

All of his maneuvers in this battle conformed to the principles of war. He did not make a flank march in the presence of the enemy because the two armies could not see each other drawn up in order of battle. The Austrian army, which would know of the approach of the Prussians by the combats of Neumarkt and Borne, waited to see it take position on the heights opposite its own line of battle, and during this time, protected by a hill and fog and masked by his advance guard, the King continued his march and arrived to attack the extreme left of the Austrian army.

Nor did he violate a second principle no less sacred—"never abandon your line of operation." But he changed his line of operation, which is considered the most skillful maneuver in the art of war. In effect an army that changes its line of operation deceives the enemy, who no longer knows the location of the opponent's rear and those sensitive points that he might threaten.

By this march Frederick abandoned the line of operation from Neumarkt and took that of Upper Silesia. The boldness and speed of execution, the bravery of the generals and soldiers matched the skill of the maneuver. For here Daun, once engaged, did everything possible and yet he did not succeed. Three times he attempted to refuse his left and center by a "left to the rear in line of battle." He even had his right advance to harass the line of operation from Neumarkt, which he assumed was still that of the King.

He did everything that was prescribed in similar circumstances. But the cavalry and the Prussian masses constantly got to his troops before they had time to form themselves. It is true also to note that Frederick was marvelously served by circumstance: all of the inferior troops, those of the empire, were on the left of the Austrian army, and the difference in quality of troops is immense.[19]

In the invasion of Saxony in 1756 . . . Frederick disregarded several principles of war that one rarely violates with impunity; that is what caused him to fail despite the gain from one battle.[20]

This Great Captain is reproached for not having profited, as he should have, from the initiative that he had displayed in 1756; for not having dealt any great blows during the spring of the next five years, when the Russians were far from the field of operations; for the faults that led to the disaster of Hochkirch, Maxen, and Landshut; and finally, for the poor directions given to his two invasions of Bohemia and that of Moravia.

But these flaws are eclipsed by his great actions, brilliant maneuvers, and bold resolutions that enabled him to emerge victorious from such an uneven struggle. He was great especially during the most critical moments: that is the greatest praise one can make on his character.

But everything indicates that he could not have resisted a campaign against France, Austria, and Russia had these powers acted in good faith. He could not even have waged two campaigns against Austria and Russia had the cabinet at St. Petersburg permitted its armies to winter in the field of operations. The marvels of the Seven Years' War then would disappear.

But what is genuine justifies the reputation that the Prussian army has enjoyed during the last fifty years of the previous century, and consolidates rather than weakens Frederick's great military reputation.[21]

Frederick's success during this war has been attributed to a novel order of tactics that he had invented called the *oblique order.* During the Seven Years' War Frederick fought ten battles in person and his lieutenants fought six, including the affairs of Maxen and Landshut. Of the former, Frederick won seven and lost three; of the battles fought by his lieutenants he lost five and won one. In sixteen battles Prussia won eight and lost eight. In none of them did the King employ a new tactic. He did nothing that had not been practiced by the ancient and modern generals over the centuries.

So what, then, is the oblique order?

Its partisans differ. Some say that all the maneuvers that an army makes on the eve or the day of battle in order to reinforce its right, center, or left, or even to move behind the enemy, belongs to the oblique order. If this be so, then Cyrus maneuvered in the oblique order at the battle of Thymbra, the Gallo-Belgians against Caesar at the battle of the Sambre, Marshal de Luxembourg at Fleurus, taking advantage of one hill to outflank the enemy's right; Marlborough at Höchstaedt, Prince Eugene at Ramillies and Turin, Charles XII at Pultowa. Indeed, there is scarcely a battle, ancient or modern, where the general who attacked did not reinforce his columns of attack either by a larger number of troops, by placing grenadiers there, or by a large number of guns. Had Frederick invented this maneuver he could have invented war, which unfortunately is as old as the world itself.

Others claim that the oblique order is that maneuver the King had performed in the Potsdam parades by which two armies at first were arrayed in parallel battle lines. The side that maneuvers against one of the wings of its adversary, either by a system of closed or open columns, and suddenly finds itself on an enemy's flank without being noticed by the opposing general, attacks the exposed wing on all sides before there is time to support it.

There are two principles of war that are not violated with impunity. The first is, "Do not make flank marches in front of an army that is in position." And the second: "Preserve your line of operation with care and never abandon it lightheartedly." Also there are those among the partisans of the oblique order who prefer that the maneuver be hidden from the enemy, executed at night, or at least favored by mists or covered by canals, so that the enemy is astonished and surprised.

Since this maneuver must be concealed from the enemy, it is not a tactical order: its strength is not in the formation itself, but in the fact that it achieves surprise. . . . It is in the nature of ambuscades, flanking marches, surprises, etc. . . .

Old Frederick laughed up his sleeve during the parades at Potsdam when he saw the infatuation of the young French, English, and Austrian officers for the oblique order, which was appropriate only for making a reputation for some battalion adjutants. A thorough investigation of the maneuvers of the Seven Years' War would have enlightened these officers and caused their illusions to evaporate. Frederick never maneuvered only by lines and by flanks, never by deployments. . . .

French admirers of the oblique order, among them Guibert, have pushed the illusion to the point of claiming that the detachments of the Duke Ferdinand at Krefeld and Wilhelmstal, on the flanks of the French army, were brilliant corollaries of the oblique order. In fact they defied the principle "Do not place any interval between the different units in your line of battle through which the enemy could penetrate." If the violation of this principle worked for him, it is because the Count de Clermont commanded the French![22]

Jomini established above all the principles. Genius acts by inspiration. What works well in one situation may be inadequate in another, but it is necessary to consider the principles as the main axis of a system, a point of reference. . . . Frederick did not attempt to say everything. He deliberately was somewhat vague in his instructions. There are so many diverse elements in war.[23]

My son should often read and meditate on history; it is the only real philosophy. And he should read and meditate on the campaigns of the Great Captains. This is the only way to learn the art of war.[24]

IV

The Combat Arms

Baron de Jomini said that "It is not so much the mode of formation as the proper combined use of the different arms which will ensure victory." Napoleon constantly adapted new drill formations and techniques to the tactical realities of the battlefield. In an age before soldiers could use improved technology to solve tactical problems, he modified and changed formations in order to achieve greater coherence, mobility, and firepower in battle.

INFANTRY

The Romans had two kinds of infantry: light infantry, which carried a missile weapon, and heavy infantry, armed with a short sword. After the invention of gunpowder, armies continued to maintain two kinds of infantry: harquebusiers, who were lightly armed and intended for scouting and harassing the enemy, and pikemen, who replaced the old heavy infantry.[1]

After the discovery of firearms a portion of the infantry continued to be armed with pikes, but the manner of placing the pikemen varied. Sometimes they were formed in the center, arrayed in six lines, with the harquebusiers placed on the flanks. Sometimes the first two ranks were composed of harquebusiers with two, three, or four ranks of pikemen in position behind them. At the beginning of 1700, Louis XIV did away with pikes and armed all of his infantry with muskets and bayonets. Infantry continued for some time, however, to form in four ranks, but they were not slow to appreciate the problem with this formation, because the fourth rank could not use its muskets. The fourth rank therefore was abolished and the formation of infantry ever since has been in three ranks.[2]

We have recognized, however, the problem of the fire of the third rank, which forces us to stipulate that the first rank place one knee on the ground when firing by platoon and by battalion. But the only fire used in war is firing at will, by the right and by the left of each platoon. Various ways have been attempted to have the third rank participate in this fire. At first we had them fire like the first two ranks, placing the barrel of the gun on the right shoulder of the man in the second rank, but because the musket barrel was only four feet eight inches long, the muzzle of the third rank scarcely extends eight inches in front of the chest of the men in the first rank and it hurt their left hand when the front rank was taking aim. There were so many accidents that it was decided to abandon the fire of the third rank as being impracticable.

Then the third rank had to load the muskets for the second rank, which no longer had anything more to do than to fire. We believed that this would increase the volume of fire, but experience has shown that the second rank fired no more than before, and did not fire as well.

The fire of skirmishers is best of all; that of a single rank comes next, that of the two ranks is still good, but the fire of three ranks is injurious. The third rank can do nothing that would increase the fire of the two ranks in front, which determines the two-rank formation for infantry.[3]

Napoleon to Marshal Marmont, 13 October 1813

I intend that you place your troops in two ranks instead of three; the third rank is of no use in firing and is of even less so for the bayonet.

When you are closed in mass, three divisions will form six ranks and three ranks of file closers. You will see the advantage that this offers: your fire will be better, your force will be increased by one third; and the enemy, accustomed to seeing us in three ranks, will overestimate our battalions to be stronger by one third than they actually are.[4]

The advantages of the formation of infantry in two ranks are:

1. That the battalions, having the rear divisions formed in square on the flanks, can bring thirty of their thirty-six muskets into action, while the battalion formed in three ranks can only use twenty-four of the thirty-six—a difference of one fourth.
2. That the front and the rear of the line of battle are flanked by the fire of fifty fusiliers, which provides more stability to this line than the presence of a third rank could offer.
3. That the flanks are protected, so that they are prepared to receive even an unexpected cavalry attack that might have masked its movement behind a knoll, whereas with the three-rank formation the battalion that is surprised by a cavalry charge on the flank is lost. . . .
4. The compact columns of half a company formed by wings will put thirty of the thirty-six muskets into action. . . .
5. In covering the fifty-four feet of two sides of the division square, which is placed in front of the line that intersects—which rarely exists—you can give a new degree of strength to the entire line.

   It is claimed that all these advantages are not exclusive to the two-rank formation, and that all can be adapted to the three-rank formation. But the latter, which reduced the fire by one third, would reduce it to . . . less than half if you were to place two divisions in reserve to the rear, and when these divisions have been placed in square on the flanks the fire will still be only slightly more than one half. . . . A battalion placed in this order would be at a serious disadvantage.[5]

Napoleon to Berthier, 22 December 1803

There will be in every battalion of light infantry regiments a company called the "mounted company" or "mobile company" or "partisan company," or some other name of this sort.

This company will always be the third in the battalion, counting the grenadier company as the first.

It will be composed of well-built and vigorous men, of the smallest height. No noncommissioned officer or soldier should be more than four feet eleven inches tall and the officers should not exceed five feet.

It will be armed with a lighter fusil than the dragoon's fusil and will be drilled in firing. Officers and noncommissioned officers will be armed with rifled carbines.

The men of these companies will be practiced in following the cavalry at a trot, holding sometimes the boot of the rider and sometimes the mane of the horse, and in mounting briskly and jumping behind the rider, so that he thus can rapidly be transported by the cavalry.

These companies will always be complete and maintained on a war footing. . . . They will be taken from among those men exempted from the conscription because they are too short.[6]

CAVALRY

The cavalry of an army in Flanders and Germany will be about one fifth; in the Alps and the Pyrenees one fifteenth, and along the coasts, one twenty-fourth.[7] In Poland war is waged with cavalry.[8] Overall the numbers of cavalry in the French army will be one sixth the strength of the infantry.[9]

Order and tactics are necessary for infantry, cavalry, artillery, scouts, chasseurs, dragoons, and cuirassiers. Cavalry has even a greater need than infantry for order and tactics. It must know how to fight dismounted and it must be drilled in the *School of the Company* and the *School of the Battalion*.[10] Infantry will never be assigned to protect it, no matter what the terrain is like. Depending upon circumstances, it will place dismounted posts in woods, among rocks, in swamps and in houses.[11] It is mere prejudice for one to assume that cavalry cannot go anywhere that infantry goes.[12] Fools will tell you that cavalry is useless in Calabria: if this is true, then cavalry is no good anywhere.[13]

The squadron will be to the cavalry what the battalion is for infantry: it will contain all of the means necessary to sustain itself and to fight. It will be commanded by a field officer, a major, and it will have a staff of ten, three companies of 130 men each, and one squad of train attendants to look after fifteen mules or draft horses. The total strength of the squadron will be 410 men.

The squadron will be organized into three companies of three platoons each, with two sections in each platoon. It will have the same formation dismounted, where it will take the same order of battle and maneuvers as a battalion wing. Three squadrons dismounted will constitute a battalion. Cavalrymen of the first and second class will have the same additional pay as their counterparts in the infantry; like the infantry, they too will be divided into gunners, sappers, and swimmers; they will carry a pioneer tool, a sandbag, and a small canvas bag and will contribute to all fieldworks along with the infantry, but in the proportion of one cavalryman for every two infantrymen.[14]

Scouts

Decree, 3 September 1802

1. Three bodies of scouts are created in the 27th military division [Turin].
2. Each body will be composed of 200 men from the infantry, sixty from the cavalry, and thirty gendarmes commanded by a field officer, and will have behind an extraordinary military commission composed of five officers and presided over by a field officer.
3. Each body of scouts will be charged with patrolling through two departments. They will go alternatively into all communities that have offered resistance to the gendarmes . . . proceed to disarm and arrest them, and have all individuals accused of

having resisted the gendarmes by force tried before an extraordinary military commission.[15]

Note Concerning the Organization of Regiments of Scouts, 9 July 1806

Prepare an organizational plan for four regiments of scouts, each comprising four squadrons of 200 men.

The height of the scouts will not exceed five feet.

The height of the horses will be from four feet to four feet three and a half inches at most.

The horses will have only the two front hoofs shoed.

The bridle will be the simplest kind possible.

They shall have a pad instead of a saddle; of course you will adapt the stirrups and other essential accessories to this pad.

The scouts will have a coat, vest, and one pair of breeches or trousers, and in addition a stable vest. They will also have a large cloak to be useful and take the place of a mantle. The valise will be as small as possible and its contents are not to exceed four pounds in weight.

The boots will be like those of the hussars, but without any decoration.

In this new branch it is my intent to utilize the small horses and to cut down on the waste of large species.

These regiments will perform the same services as scouts that have previously been performed by hussars and chasseurs. We will be able to multiply them everywhere with the greatest facility because we will be able to find horses this size at all times and nearly all places, and in the field these units will be able to remount themselves with all kinds of horses.

As a consequence of this new organization, men under five feet in height and therefore too small to serve in the dragoons can be utilized in the cavalry, just like they are already used in the infantry with the creation of *voltigeur* companies, and therefore these regiments will be proportionately far less expensive. . . .

The horses of the scouts would be maintained at all times in the open air and fed on the meadow, without oats. This is a worthwhile experiment, for it causes no inconvenience to France for eight or nine months out of the year. However, during the three or four winter months this experiment must be modified in nearly all of France because of heavy frosts and snow. In my opinion it will be indispensable to have sheds closed on two or three sides in place of pasture, and to feed the horses dry fodder as long as the heavy cold or snow persists. . . .

I have decided on the proposed plan because of the above considerations, and also by what I have seen in the Army of Italy and the Army of Egypt.[16]

The scouts are a part of the battalions and are always under the orders of infantry officers. They are commanded only by lieutenants so that, reunited with cavalry temporarily after charges or pursuits, these lieutenants cannot in any event outrank captains of cavalry. They will maneuver with their battalion, from which they will never be separated. The aide-de-camp of the brigadier and the major (chef d'escadron) responsible for inspecting them will command them only when, as a result of a charge or a mission, they find themselves separated from their battalions.

Officers, noncommissioned officers, and soldiers will be dismounted and remounted according to the will of the major, who will use them for grenadiers and *voltigeurs.* They will not be employed in any of the maneuver combinations of cavalry, for which the small size of their horses makes them unsuitable. No man can participate in a company of scouts who has not served at least one year in the *voltigeurs,* if he is not less than five feet one inch in height, and if he does not have very good vision.

In time of war officers and noncommissioned officers will be taken as much as possible from among the men who understand the language of the country where the war is being waged, or who are familiar with the enemy army. They will provide the disposition of troops for battle to the general officers . . . of their division, escort prisoners, and baggage, and provide relays.

Because of all these functions they will be considered as cavalry, for in fact today this service employs a large number of chasseurs, hussars, dragoons, and cuirassiers. The small size of the horses of scouts makes them especially capable of following infantry everywhere, and that has the additional advantage for our country to economize the expenses of remounting.[17]

Chasseurs and Hussars

Light horse will constitute the light cavalry of the army and will be armed with a carbine and a bayonet weighing less than six pounds, a saber of the same model as the chasseurs of the Guard, weighing less than three pounds, and with two pistols weighing less than one pound each and attached to the saddle tree by straps. In addition, half of the men in the squadron will be armed with a lance and none will have any defensive arms other than the scaled epaulettes and an iron cross on the shakos.

They will be trained to cross rivers by swimming beside their horses, grasping them by the mane, and holding the carbine above the water. The horses will be harnessed as simply as possible. They are expected to be able to drink while bridled and will be accustomed to watering only once a day. The accoutrement of the men will be simple, large, and comfortable. Officers, noncommissioned officers, and soldiers will always sleep fully clothed, in peacetime as well as in war.[18]

Light cavalry should cover the front of the army at a great distance; therefore it cannot belong to the infantry. It should be supported and protected especially by cavalry of the line. At all times there should be useful rivalry and emulation between the infantry and cavalry. Light cavalry is necessary to the advance guard, the rear guard, and on the flanks of the army, therefore it cannot be attached to any particular infantry corps in order to follow its movements.

It would be more natural to combine the administration of light cavalry with that of cavalry of the line than to make it depend on that of the infantry, with which it has much less in common.[19] The esprit of the regiment and its administration should be one.[20] It must, however, have its own administration.[21]

Cavalry requires more officers than infantry, and therefore it must be better instructed. For it is not only speed that assures its success, but order, cohesion, and the effective use of its reserves. If light cavalry must form the advance guard, then it is necessary for it to be organized into squadrons, brigades, and divisions so that it can maneuver, because the advance guards and rear guards do nothing else. They pursue or fall back in formation somewhat similar to a chessboard[22]; they form themselves into several lines or deploy into column, perform a rapid change of front to outflank an entire wing or the entire enemy army. It is by virtue of the combination of all these evolutions that a numerically inferior advance or rear guard can avoid actions that are too vigorous, or a general engagement, yet at the same time can delay the enemy long enough for the army to arrive, the infantry to deploy, the commanding general to make his dispositions, and the baggage trains and the park to move forward.

The art of a general commanding the advance or the rear guard is to pursue the enemy or to keep him at arm's length, to contain him, delay him, and to force him to spend three or four hours in advancing a league, without compromising your own forces. Tactics alone provide the means of achieving these great results, and therefore it is more essential to have cavalry than infantry in the advance guard—or the rear guard—than in any other position.

The Hungarian insurrection that we saw in 1797, 1805, and 1809 was pitiful. If these light troops in the days of [the Empress] Maria Theresa made themselves formidable, it was because of their good organization and especially their large numbers.[23]

But to assume that similar troops were superior to Wurmser's hussars or the dragoons of Latour and the Archduke John is to have a strange notion of things. Neither the Hungarian insurrection nor the Cossacks have ever formed the advance guards like the Austrian or Russian armies, because whoever speaks of advance guard has in mind troops that maneuver. The Russians consider one regiment of trained Cossacks the equivalent of three untrained regiments. Everything would be contemptible about these troops were it not for the Cossack himself—a handsome man, strong, adroit, shrewd, a skilled rider and indefatigable. Born on a horse and reared in civil wars, he is for the plains what the Bedouin is on the desert and the Barbet in the Alps. . . .

Two Mamelukes would keep three Frenchmen at bay because they are better armed, better mounted, better drilled, and have two pairs of pistols, a blunderbuss, a carbine, a helmet with visor, a coat of mail, several horses, and several footmen to serve them. But 100 French cavalry need not fear 100 Mamelukes, 300 would not fear 400 Mamelukes, 600 would not fear 900, and ten squadrons would put 2,000 Mamelukes to flight—such is the controlling influence of tactics, formation, and of the drill evolutions! [In Egypt] the cavalry generals Murat, Lasalle, and Leclerc appeared before the Mamelukes in three lines and a reserve; just as the first line was at the verge of being outflanked the second moved forward by squadron to the right and to the left into line. The Mamelukes stopped abruptly to outflank this second line, which, as soon as it was extended by the third, charged them. They could not stand up against the shock and they dispersed.

It is a contradiction to desire to bring together several thousand light cavalry, to earmark it for the advance guard or the rear guard of an army, and still not want it to be instructed in maneuvers of the line. The movements of an advance or a rear guard do not consist in advancing or withdrawing at a gallop, but in maneuvering, and for that you need good light cavalry, good reserves of cavalry of the line, excellent infantry battalions, and good light batteries. The troops must know their tactics equally well, each according to the demands of his rank and his arm.

It is recognized that for facility in maneuvers the squadron should contain 100 men and that three or four squadrons should be led by a major.[24]

Heavy Cavalry: Dragoons

Light cavalry and dragoons . . . are two entirely different arms. One dragoon regiment by itself can do nothing, but four or five regiments together, 2,000 strong, maneuvering flawlessly on foot, will be very useful.[25]

All cavalry of the line should not be armed with a cuirass. Dragoons, mounted on horses four feet nine inches in height, armed with a straight saber, without breastplates, should belong to the heavy cavalry. They must be armed with an infantry musket with bayonet, have the infantry shako, a pair of trousers overlapping the laced half-boots, cloaks with sleeves and valise so small that they can carry them as shoulder belts.

The dragoon squadron will be divided into three companies, each comprising 120 dragoons and ten scouts. These scouts will be provided by the infantry as soon as the squadron takes the field: they will serve as horse holders when the dragoons fight dismounted. The scouts will provide orderlies to generals and field officers, and escort prisoners and the baggage. Dragoons will never be assigned to these duties.

The dragoon will have a very light boot so as not to be encumbered on foot. His valise will be so small that if necessary he could carry it on foot. He will be armed with a musket with bayonet, called "the dragoon musket." His cartridge box will contain sixty rounds, but he will place only fifteen rounds in it when he is mounted—the remaining forty-five rounds will be divided around the pistol holster and placed in the cartridge box at the command "Prepare to Fight. Dismount!"

His saber will be straight like that of the cuirassiers, and his head gear and accoutrements will resemble those of the infantry as closely as possible, so that from a distance it would be difficult to distinguish him from the infantry when he is dismounted in battle. In advance and rear guards the dragoon will provide dismounted posts jointly with infantry, but in the proportion of one to four, not including the scouts.[26]

Turenne, Prince Eugene of Savoy, and the Duke de Vendôme had a high opinion of dragoons and made great use of them. This arm covered itself with glory in Italy in 1795, 1796, and 1797, as well as in Egypt and Spain. The campaigns of 1806 and 1807 gave rise to a prejudice against dragoons that is not deserved. Dragoon divisions had been assembled at Compiègne and Amiens to be embarked without horses for the expedition to England, where they were to serve on foot until they could be mounted on local horses. General Baraguay d'Hilliers, their first inspector, commanded them. He made them perform as foot soldiers and incorporated a large number of recruits, whom he had drilled only in infantry maneuvers. No longer were they real cavalry regiments. In 1806 they campaigned on foot until after the battle of Jena, when they were mounted on horses captured from the Prussian cavalry, three fourths of which were unfit. These combined circumstances hurt the dragoons.

Dragoons are necessary to support the light cavalry with the advance guard, the rear guard, and on the flanks of the army. Cuirassiers are less fit to perform this duty because of their breastplates. It is necessary, however, to have some of them in the advance guard, if only to accustom them to war and keep them going. One division of 1,600 dragoons can move swiftly to a point with 1,500 light cavalry horses, dismount there to defend a bridge, the head of a defile, or commanding terrain, and then hold on until the infantry arrives.

You can imagine the advantages of this arm during a retreat.[27]

Cuirassiers

I could not recommend too highly the instruction of my cuirassiers. . . . This arm, which has rendered me such important services, needs to be well instructed. One could say that instruction does everything. The Russian cavalry did not lack courage [at Austerlitz], and still it has nearly been all massacred, and my Guard has lost nobody.[28]

You know that cuirassiers are of greater use than all other cavalry.[29] My intention is that the heavy cavalry be always on a war footing. . . . It is in the heavy cavalry that the science of the mounted man should be carried to the highest degree.[30] Cuirassiers must be large men . . . consequently they require large horses.[31]

Napoleon to General Clarke, 12 November 1811

I respond to your letter of the 6th regarding the armament of cuirassiers and lancers. This is an extremely important question.

It is acknowledged that cavalry armed with a cuirass can use the carbine only with difficulty, but it is no less absurd for 3,000 or 4,000 such brave men to be caught by surprise in their cantonment or delayed in their march by two companies of *voltigeurs*. It is therefore essential to arm them. In the *ancien régime* cuirassier regiments had carbines that they carried, not slung across the back like light cavalry, but in such a way to be used as muskets.

I wish you to form a committee of cavalry officers and make a decision on this subject. I cannot get used to seeing 3,000 elite men who, in an insurrection or a surprise by light troops, would be wiped out by a partisan, or stopped on a march by some inferior marksmen behind some stream or house. This is absurd.

My intention is that each man will have a musket, that it be a very short carbine, carried in the most convenient way for cuirassiers—exactly how, it does not much matter. I have already had carbines issued to the heavy cavalry. During peace they have refused them, and in the most recent campaign they have not had any.

Prepare a plan . . . so that these 3,000 men have no need of infantry to guard them in their cantonments, and, dismounting, can break out when a disproportionately small force of infantry blocks them. . . . War consists of unforeseen events, not in having assumptions that 15,000 heavy cavalry must always be kept in such a way as to be protected.

As for lancers, see if it is possible to give them a carbine with their lance. If this is not possible, it would be necessary at least to have a third of the company armed with carbines, that is to say, the entire first rank and half of the second, and all quartermasters and a third of the company (nearly forty men, assuming full ranks) armed with carbines. Cossacks have the lance, but they have carbines and even muskets with which they fire at great distance.[32]

The cuirassier squadron will be composed of three divisions, each of 125 cuirassiers and ten scouts to provide orderlies to the field officers, escort prisoners, and to hold the horses when the cuirassiers fight dismounted. The cuirassier will be armed with carbine with bayonet, a pair of pistols, and a straight saber. He will carry fifteen cartridges around the pistol holders and will not have a cartridge box. When forced to fight dismounted, he will place them in his right pocket and he will receive from the park fifteen additional cartridges, which he will put in his pocket. He will keep the hooded cape.

Cuirassiers will be especially placed in reserve to support the light cavalry and dragoons. They will never be placed with the advance guards, rear guards, or wings, except when it is necessary to accustom them to the hardships of war or to assist the dragoons.

The cavalry brigade, whether light cavalry, dragoons, or cuirassiers, will be composed of three squadrons and comprise 1,230 men. It will be commanded by a brigadier general having the same staff as a brigadier general of infantry. The division will consist of two brigades, or 2,460 men . . . and when the cavalry of the army will be formed of only 3,000 to 4,000 men, one could compose the division with a brigade of each arm.

A cavalry wing will be composed of three divisions—one of light cavalry, one of dragoons, and one of cuirassiers. Each . . . will have a battery of light artillery of six 6-pounders and two howitzers. The cavalry wing will have an effective of 7,380 horses and twenty-eight guns.[33]

You should regard cuirassiers, dragoons, and hussars as forming three different arms and that . . . officers of these units should never transfer from one arm to another.[34] That strikes me as a practice that has all kinds of drawbacks.[35]

Artillery

The organization of the artillery is the most urgent, because of all the combat arms it always requires much more time to get ready.[36] It is always the artillery that holds up the formation of armies.[37]

Only with cannon can one wage war.[38] Great battles are won with artillery.[39] It may be true that good infantry is the nerve of the army, but if it has to fight for long against superior artillery it would become demoralized and be destroyed. . . . No infantry, however brave, can march 3,000 or 3,600 feet with impunity against sixteen or twenty-four well-placed guns, served by good gunners. Before it would get two thirds of the way its men would be killed, wounded, or scattered. Field artillery has acquired too much accuracy in its fire for us to agree with Machiavelli, who, enamored of the ideas of the Greeks and Romans, wanted to make only one discharge of artillery before withdrawing it behind his line of battle.[40]

The formation and function of artillery . . . profoundly influences our modern tactics for success in battle, and almost exclusively it dominates the capture and defense of modern fortresses.[41] In siege warfare, as in the field, artillery plays the principal role: it has wrought a complete revolution.[42] It is artillery that takes the fortified cities—infantry can only give assistance.[43]

In the initial campaigns of the war of the Revolution, France always excelled in the artillery. I cannot think of a single example in this war where twenty guns, suitably posted, were seized *à la baïonnette* by infantry alone. At the affair of Valmy, the battle of Jemappes, and at Noerdlingen and Fleurus in 1792, our artillery was superior to that of the enemy, although often we had only two guns per thousand men simply because our army was so large. It was generally better drilled and more skilled than its adversary, having at hand better infantry, and it obtained success during a part of the campaign even though its artillery park was much inferior. But on the decisive day of a general engagement, it will cruelly feel its inferiority in artillery and will run the risk of losing everything in an instant.[44]

My system of regular war requires a large quantity of artillery.[45] Everywhere a regiment goes you need artillery.[46] You must have as much artillery as your enemy, based upon four guns per 1,000 infantry and cavalry. The better the infantry, the greater the need to be careful of it and support it with good batteries. The greatest part of the artillery should be with the infantry and cavalry divisions, the smallest portion in reserve. Each gun should have 300 rounds with it, not counting the small chest. That is the normal expenditure for two battles.[47]

Napoleon to Marshal Davout, 10 May 1811

I have ordered that your artillery be completed for five divisions and composed as follows:

Two reserve batteries, served by the fort artillery, each comprising two long-range howitzers and six 12-pounders;

Five batteries of horse artillery (one per division), each of two howitzers and four 6-pounders;

Five batteries of foot artillery, each of two howitzers and six 6-pounders; and finally

Two batteries of horse artillery for the cuirassiers.

This makes twenty-eight howitzers, twelve 12-pounders, and fifty-eight 6-pounders, a total of ninety-eight guns. Added to the sixty-four guns of the corps trains, this makes a total of 162 guns. By this means your five divisions will be organized. The number of wagons will therefore be 992. You must have only two train battalions.[48]

If you have only six guns for each division that is not enough. You need a dozen. One wages war with artillery.[48]

Every day convinces me of the great damage that has been done to our armies by removing the regimental guns. I desire therefore that in the organization, each regiment will have two 3-pounders; but, during the time that we should have only guns and ammunition for 4-pounders, you will give them 4-pounders. The gunners, horses, and men of the train will be supplied by the regiments.[49]

Never forget that in war all artillery must be with the army and not in the park.[50] Had I possessed 30,000 artillery rounds at Leipzig on the evening of 18 October, today I would be master of the world.[51]

THE ARTILLERY OFFICER

It is necessary to be familiar with artillery . . . [and] I believe that every officer ought to serve in the artillery, which is the arm that can produce most of the good generals. . . . To be a good general you must know mathematics; it serves to direct your thinking in a thousand circumstances.[52]

The artillery staff must serve with greater activity on the battlefield. It is up to the artillery commander and staff officers to place the guns in position and to withdraw them, to anticipate the expenditure of ammunition, to correct poor sites that the company officers select, and finally to have artillery perform the duty that it has always done with such distinction.[53]

The best generals will be those who move up from the field artillery.[54] It is the duty of an artillery general to understand all of the operations of the army, insofar as he is forced to provide the different divisions with arms and ammunition. His contacts with the individual battery commander in each division enable him to know everything that is going on.[55]

Notes on a Plan of Regulations for the Artillery and Engineer School, 27 June 1801

The total length of the course of the school being fixed at two years, we must divide the course into four parts, each comprising six months of study. Students in the first class would learn:

1. the infantry maneuvers of the platoon and battalion
2. the maneuvers of field and siege artillery as well as those of mortars and howitzers
3. mechanical maneuvers, the composition of explosives . . .
4. the principles of the attack of fortifications
5. the entire portion of the *aide-mémoire* pertaining to firing, and finally
6. everything necessary to the gunner and the engineer in the field.

Students will be led to the target range; they will lob bombs into the target barrel, fire blank cartridges, etc., and construct every kind of battery. They will continue their [initial] course of construction.

In the third class students would pursue their studies in hydraulic architecture, civil and military. They would busy themselves with the most complicated part of construction and learn everything necessary to direct and superintend the construction of a fort. They would take cognizance of the details of foundries, mines, etc.

The fourth class would be dedicated to perfecting the students in the different subjects that they have been studying. They would go over all of the details of arsenals, mines, galleries, etc.—in brief, everything that would complete their instruction as engineers and gunners would belong to the curriculum of this class. . . .

In general, in the establishment of a school for engineers and artillery one should consider the knowledge of the maneuvers of all the guns and the tactics of infantry as the principal object. When a student is admitted to the *School of the Battalion,* he would be forced to perform the manual of arms and the maneuvers of the battalion at least three times every ten days.

It is important for the maneuvers of artillery to keep in mind that nothing is more uncertain than the art of firing. This portion of the military art is classified among the physio-mathematical sciences, yet its results are dubious; those of practice are certain. Students having completed one course in mechanics know nearly everything that they must understand and apply.

It is appropriate therefore to strive above everything else, and not as one of the foremost foundations of the instruction, to see that each student executes the manual of arms and all of the maneuvers of artillery better than a veteran soldier, that he is skilled in large practice and has perfect knowledge of the employment of artillery. No one can be considered a good student if, upon graduation, he cannot go immediately to a battery or a siege. It is proper that upon joining his unit he should instruct a class of recruits in the maneuvers of artillery and infantry and in the mechanical maneuvers. How often do you not see officers unable to place a gun carriage, direct a mechanical maneuver, fashion explosives, and forced to take lessons from old sergeants?

When a student can aim a gun better than the soldier, no one will question either his right to advancement or the other advantages of his education. Old sergeants will not be jealous of these young officers when they never have to teach them anything.[56]

Generalship and the Art of Command

"It is essential that a general should dissemble while appearing to be occupied, working with the mind and working with the body, ceaselessly suspicious while affecting tranquillity, saving of his soldiers and not squandering them except for the most important interests, informed of everything, always on the lookout to deceive the enemy and careful not to be deceived himself. In a word he should be more than an industrious, active, and indefatigable man, but one who does not forget one thing to execute another, and above all who does not despise those little details which pertain to great projects."

—*Frederick the Great,*
Instructions to His Generals, *1747*

In war men are nothing; one man is everything.[1] The presence of the general is indispensable. He is the head, the whole of an army. It was not the Roman army that subdued Gaul, but Caesar; not the Carthaginian army that caused the republic to tremble at the gates of Rome, but Hannibal; not the Macedonian army that reached the Indus, but Alexander; not the French army that carried the war to the Weser and the Inn, but Turenne; and not the Prussian army that defended Prussia for seven years against the three greatest powers of Europe, but Frederick the Great. . . . [2] In war only the commander understands the importance of certain things, and he alone, through his will and superior insight, conquers and surmounts all difficulties.[3] An army is nothing without the head.[4]

Since the war depends absolutely on the season, each month requires a different plan of campaign. The government must place entire confidence in its general, allow him great latitude and put forward only the objective he is to fulfill.[5] A commander is not protected by an order from a minister or a prince who is absent from the theater of operations and has little or no knowledge of the most recent turn of events. Every commander responsible for executing a plan that he considers bad or disastrous is criminal: he must point out the flaws, insist that it be changed, and at last resort resign rather than be the instrument of the destruction of his own men. Every commander in chief who, as a result of superior orders, delivers a battle convinced that he will lose it, is likewise criminal.

A general in chief is the top officer in the chain of command. The minister or prince gives instructions to which he must adhere—both in spirit and in conscience—but these instructions are never military orders and do not require passive obedience. Even a direct military order requires only passive obedience when it is given by a superior who, being present at the time he gives it, knows the condition of affairs and can listen to the objections and provide explanations to those who must execute the order. . . .

The conduct of the Duke d'Orléans before Turin in 1706 has been justified: historians have cleared him of all blame. The Duke d'Orléans was prince, he had been regent, and he was of an easygoing disposition. The writers have treated him favorably, while Marchin, resting dead on the battlefield, could not defend himself. We know, however, that as he lay dying he protested the decision to remain in the lines.

But who was the commander of the French army in Italy? The Duke d'Orléans, Marchin, la Feuillade, and Albergotti were all under his orders. It was up to him whether or not he would take the advice of a counsel of war; he was in the chair. It was his decision whether or not to conform to the opinion of the war council. The prince did not have trouble in his command. Nobody refused to obey him. Had he given the order for the army to leave its lines, if he could give the order to the left to cross the Dora to reinforce the right; if he could have given the positive order to Albergotti to recross the Po, and the generals had refused to obey under the pretext that they did not owe him obedience, then all would be well and good. The prince would be exonerated. But, it is argued, Albergotti did not obey the order that he received to send a detachment to the right bank of the Po. He settled for making observations.

Well, that happens every day. It does not in itself constitute an act of disobedience. Had the prince sent him a positive order . . . it would have been obeyed. . . . The Duke d'Orléans was recognized as commander in chief by the generals, officers, and men. None refused—or could have refused—to obey him. He is responsible for all that was done.

General Jourdan states in his *Mémoires* that the government had pressured him into fighting the battle of Stockach and he seeks thus to justify himself for the unfortunate consequences of this affair. But this justification could not be allowed even when he had received a positive and formal order, as we have demonstrated. When he decided to deliver battle, he believed that he had favorable chances to win it. He deceived himself.

But, might it not happen that a minister or prince should explain his intentions so clearly that no clause could be misunderstood and that he says to a commander: "Deliver battle; the enemy, by virtue of his numbers, the quality of his troops, and the position that he occupies will defeat you. No matter—this is my will."

Should such an order be passively executed? No! If the general understands the benefit and consequently the morality of so strange an order, *he* must execute it. If he does not understand it, however, he should not obey.

Something of this sort often occurs in war. A battalion is left in a difficult position to save the army, but the battalion commander receives the positive order from his superior, who is present at the time he gives it and responds to all objections, if there are reasonable ones to make. It is a military order given by a commander who is present and to whom one owes passive obedience. But what happens if the minister or prince is with the army? Then he takes over command, he is the commander in chief. The previous commander is no more than a subordinate division commander.

It does not follow that a commander in chief must not obey a minister who orders him to give battle. On the contrary, he must do it every time that, in his judgment, the chances and probabilities are as much for as against him, for our observation only applies in the case where the chances appear to be entirely against him.[6]

Unity of Command

Unity of command is of the first necessity in war. You must keep the army united, concentrate as many of your troops as possible on the battlefield, and take advantage of every opportunity, for fortune is a woman: if you miss her today, do not expect to find her tomorrow.[7]

Napoleon to the Executive Directory, 14 May 1796

I believe it very impolitic to divide the Army of Italy in two; it is likewise contrary to the interests of the republic to place two different generals in command.

The expedition to Livorno, Rome, and Naples is a mere trifle; it must be made by divisions in echelons so that by a retrograde march one could move in force against the Austrians and threaten to envelop them at the slightest movement that they might make.

For that you need not only a single general, but even more important, nothing should hinder him in his march and his operations. I waged the campaign without consulting anyone. I could not have done it well had I been forced to reconcile my point of view with that of another. I won advantages over far superior forces and with a pressing shortage of everything because, convinced that I had your confidence, my march was as quick as my thoughts. . . . If you weaken your means by dividing your forces, or break the unity of military thought in Italy . . . you will have lost the most favorable occasion for imposing laws on Italy.

In the posture of affairs of the republic in Italy, it is indispensable that you have one general who possesses your complete confidence. If it is not me I shall not complain in useless repetition, but redouble my zeal to earn your esteem in the position that you confide to me. Each man has his style of waging war. General Kellermann has more experience and will do it better than I, but the two of us together would be a disaster.[8]

It would be better to have one poor general than two good ones. War, like government, is a matter of tact.[9]

Great operations . . . require speed in movements and as much quickness in conception as in execution. . . . We require therefore unity of thought—military, diplomatic, and financial.[10]

The Attributes of a Good Commander

The foremost quality of a commander is to keep a cool head, to receive accurate impressions of what is happening, and never fret or be amazed or intoxicated by good news or bad. The successive or simultaneous sensations that the commander's mind receives during the course of a day are classified and occupy only as much attention as they deserve, for common sense and good judgment are products of a comparison of several sensations considered. There are men who, because of their physical and moral makeup, distort a picture of everything. No matter how much knowledge, intellect, courage, and other good qualities they might have, nature has not called upon them to command armies or to direct the great operations of war.[11]

Kilmaine . . . was an excellent cavalry officer. He possessed sangfroid and the ability to take in a military situation at a glance [*coup d'oeil*]. He was very well suited to command detached corps of observation and any delicate missions that required discernment, intellect, and sound judgment. . . . He knew a great deal about the Austrian troops, was familiar with their tactics, and he never let himself be awed by the false reports that they customarily spread in the rear areas of an army, nor by the heads of columns that they throw against communications in all directions, to create the impression of large forces where there are none.[12]

The essential quality of a general is firmness . . . which is a gift from heaven.[13] [In the campaign of 1800 in Germany] Moreau, three times in forty days, repeated the same demonstrations, but every time without giving them the appearance of reality. He succeeded only in emboldening his enemy and he offered him occasions to strike the isolated divisions. . . . During this campaign the French army, which was the more numerous, was nearly always inferior in numbers on the battlefield. That is what happens to generals who are irresolute and act without principles and plans. In war tentative measures . . . lose everything.[14] Military genius is a gift from heaven . . . but the most essential quality for a general is firmness of character and the resolution to conquer at any price.[15]

In war nothing is accomplished except through calculation. Anything that is not profoundly meditated in its details will produce no result.[16] Matters are contemplated over a long period of time and, to attain success, you must devote several months to thinking about what might happen.[17] If I take so many precautions it is because my habit is to leave nothing to chance.[18]

A plan of campaign must anticipate everything that the enemy can do and contain within it the means of outmaneuvering him.[19] Plans of campaign are modified to infinity, according to circumstances, the genius of the commander, the nature of the troops, and the topography. There are two kinds of plans of campaign: good plans and bad plans. Sometimes the good plans fail as a result of accidental circumstances, and occasionally bad ones succeed through some freak of fortune.[20]

Success in war depends upon the prudence, good conduct, and experience of the general.[21] You do not require spirit in war, but exactitude, character, and simplicity.[22] The art of being sometimes audacious and sometimes very prudent is the secret of success.[23] [In 1792] Dumouriez made a very audacious move by positioning himself in the midst of the Prussian army. Even though I am a more audacious warrior than he was, I would not have dared such a maneuver.[24]

It is said that I am daring, but Frederick [the Great] was much more so. He was great especially at the most critical moments. This is the highest praise one could make of his character.[25] Caesar . . . ran great risks in adventures where he demonstrated his boldness. He extracted himself from them through his genius. . . . He was at one and the same time a man of great genius and great audacity.[26] Turenne is the only general whose boldness increased with age and experience. . . . His last campaigns are superb.[27]

Marshal Ney . . . is a brave man, zealous and all heart.[28] [At Waterloo] he was given the honor of commanding the great attack in the center. It could not have been entrusted to a braver man or one more accustomed to this sort of affair.[29] Admirable for his bravery and stubbornness in retreats, he was good when it came to leading 10,000 men, but with a larger force he was a real fool. . . . Always the first under fire, he forgot about troops who were not under his immediate command.[30]

I loved Murat because of his brilliant bravery, which is why I put up with so much of his foolishness. Like Ney, Murat was incomparable on the field of battle, but he always committed stupid mistakes. He understood how to conduct a campaign better than Ney and still he was a poor general. He always waged war without maps, and how many mistakes did he not commit to be able to establish his headquarters in a château where there could be women![31] As for bedding down with a woman . . . my woman could have died in Munich or Strasbourg and it would not have upset my projects or views by a quarter of an hour.[32]

Intelligent and intrepid generals assure the success of actions.[33] One must be slow in deliberation and quick in execution.[34] To win is not enough: it is necessary to profit from success.[35] In the profession of war, like that of letters, each has his style. For sharp, prolonged attacks that require great boldness Masséna would be more appropriate than Reynier. To protect the kingdom against invasion, Jourdan is preferable to Masséna.[36] General Reynier . . . had been trained to be a topographical engineer. He understood maps thoroughly, had waged campaigns with the armies of the North and of the Rhine, where he acquired the reputation of being a man of sound advice, but he lacked the most essential qualities of a commander in chief. He loved solitude, was by nature cold and silent and not very communicative, and he knew neither how to electrify or to dominate men.[37]

A division commander in the Army of Italy, Masséna . . . had a strong constitution and was tireless, on his horse night and day among the boulders and in the mountains. This was the kind of war that he understood particularly well. He was determined, brave, bold, full of ambition and vanity. His distinctive characteristic was stubbornness, and he never got discouraged. He would neglect discipline and pay little attention to administration, and for this reason was not much loved by the soldiers. He was tolerably poor in his dispositions for an attack. His conversation was not very interesting, but at the first cannon shot, in the midst of bullets and dangers, his thought would acquire strength and clarity. If defeated he would start again as if he had been the victor.[38]

[Lannes] was wise, prudent and bold. In the presence of the enemy he possessed imperturbable sangfroid. He had little education but real natural ability. On the battlefield he was superior to all of the French generals when it came to maneuvering 15,000 men. He was still young and he would have continued to improve; perhaps he would have been clever even at Grand Tactics.[39]

Berthier, the chief of staff, always spent the day around me in combat and the night at his desk: it is impossible to combine more activity, goodwill, courage, and knowledge.[40] He was very active and followed his general on all reconnaissances without neglecting any of his work at the bureau. He possessed an indecisive character and was little fit for command, but he had all the qualities of a good chief of staff. He knew topography well, understood reconnaissance detachments, attended personally to the expedition of orders, and was accustomed to briefing the most complicated movements of an army with simplicity.[41]

Desaix was the most capable of commanding large armies. Better than the others, he understood *la grande guerre* as I understand it. In my judgment Kléber was second in this respect, and Lannes perhaps third.[42]

Moreau had no system in either politics or military matters. An excellent soldier, he was personally brave and very capable of moving a small army on the battlefield, but he was an absolute stranger to the knowledge of Grand Tactics.[43] Without his woman he could have performed admirably for me, for basically he was a brave man, but he could not effectively command more than 20,000 men. This was the opinion of Kléber and Desaix. Perhaps under my tutelage he would have been molded. With 40,000 men I would not fear Moreau with 60,000—or Jourdan with 100,000![44]

Henry IV was a good soldier, but in his time war demanded only courage and good sense. It was very different in a war fought with great masses.[45] The bravery that a commander in chief must display differs from that required of a division commander, since his bravery should not resemble that of a grenadier captain.[46] Glory and the honor of arms is the first duty that a general who delivers battle must consider; the safety and conservation of his men is only secondary. But it is also in his boldness and stubbornness that the safety and conservation of men is found.[47]

In war good health is indispensable.[48] For it is at night when the commander must do his work. If he tires himself unduly during the day fatigue will overcome him at night. At Vitoria we were defeated because Joseph [Bonaparte] slept too much. Had I slept the night before Eckmühl I would never have carried out this superb maneuver, which is the most beautiful that I have ever made. . . . My activity enabled me to be everywhere. . . . A commander should not sleep.[49]

War is waged only with vigor, decision, and unshaken will. One must neither grope nor hesitate.[50] I have very rarely met with that "two o'clock in the morning courage"; in other words, spontaneous courage which is necessary on some unexpected occasion and which permits full freedom of judgment and decision despite the most unforeseen events.[51]

In war the first principle of the commander is to conceal what he is doing, to see if there are ways of overcoming the obstacles, and to do everything toward this end once he has made his decision.[52] One sees only his own problems and not those of the enemy. It is essential to display confidence.[53]

But the generals are not content if they do not have an entire army.[54] They are always making requests—it is in the nature of things. There is not one who can be trusted in that respect. It is quite natural that the man charged with only one responsibility focuses entirely on that. The more troops, the better assurance of success. One makes a great mistake to consider their requests if it is not likely to be honored.[55]

One always has enough troops when he knows how to use them

and when the generals do not sleep in the towns but instead bivouac with their troops.[56]

The loss of time is irreparable in war. The reasons that one gives are always poor, because operations misfire only through delays.[57] The art consists simply in gaining time when one has inferior forces.[58]

Napoleon to Marshal Bessières, 20 November 1809

I notice with pain that you do not march with suitable energy. You are commander in chief; you must remove all difficulties. . . . Everything you do will be well done provided you are soon victorious. March rapidly and vigorously *without any but, if, or because.* The special affection that I have for you has caused me to decide to let you acquire this glory. Be of firm character and will. . . . Overcome all obstacles. I will disapprove your actions only if they are fainthearted and irresolute. Everything that is vigorous, firm, and discreet will meet with my approval.[59]

Orders

When you issue orders, take measures to assure that they are executed and punish those who commit such a serious fault. Why repeat an order? An order must always be carried out; when it is not, it is a crime and the guilty man must be punished.[60]

Give your orders in such a way that they cannot be disobeyed. . . . Carefully explain . . . that they are not susceptible of any but, if, or because; and that twenty-four hours after the orders are received these regiments must be on the move.[61]

Napoleon to Marshal Berthier, 9 July 1812

The Emperor cannot give you positive orders, but only general instructions because the distance is already considerable and will become greater still. . . . The first objective for your corps is to protect the Niemen, so that the navigation on it cannot be disturbed in any way. Your second objective is to contain the garrison of Riga; the third, to threaten to cross the Dvina between Riga and Dinabourg in order to harass the enemy; the fourth, to occupy Courland and to keep the country intact, since the enemy finds so many resources for his army there; and finally, as soon as the right moment has arrived, to cross the Dvina, blockade Riga, bring up the siege equipage and begin the siege of this fortress, which is important for us to possess in order to assure our winter quarters and give us a *point d'appui* on this large stream.[62]

The conduct of generals is more delicate after battles than before because then, having been able to pursue only one course, they find themselves criticized by everybody who favored other alternatives. As for me, I apply myself to follow the spirit of the instruction of the government and if, by the swiftness of events, the force of circumstances and the distance involved, I have taken something on myself, this has only been with the greatest repugnance. . . . In military operations I consult nobody; in diplomatic operations I consult everybody.[63]

In an army corps the eye of the commander must remedy everything. Captains and officers, whatever their merits might be in other respects, are constantly in a state of carelessness if the presence of the commander does not continually make itself felt.[64]

VI

Army Organization

"It is only progressively that one can form a great army," commented Sir Ian Hamilton in 1921. Certainly no other commander in his day devoted as much thought and attention to organization as Napoleon, who went into painstaking detail to assure that his forces were disciplined, prepared, and ready to take the field. "The army," he insisted, "marches, works, and has its being by organization and discipline."

A great army can be formed only by stages.[1] The organization should progress one step at a time.[2] When a nation has no cadres or principle of military organization, it is very difficult for it to organize an army. If France in 1790 managed to raise good armies so promptly, it was only because it had a good foundation which the flight of the aristocrats improved rather than made worse.[3]

The organization of the armies of Louis XIV was vicious: had today's organization existed at the battle of Fontenoy, the maneuvers would not have been piecemeal. And when Turenne declared that "an army should not exceed 50,000 men," we must understand what he meant by "army": in his day an army was not organized by divisions. The commander had to direct everything. It was necessary for him to appoint generals to command the various units, and in such a case it is easy to understand why, if he was to see everything in front of him and command by himself, he feared confusion if he had more than 50,000 men. But he did not contend that with 50,000 men he would have the advantage over an army of 200,000. He would have said that in this case he would have several armies—comparable to our divisions and army corps of today.[4]

Armies were weak in Turenne's time, which meant that fortresses had a significant role. . . . There is no position that can stop an army of 200,000 to 300,000 men, while a skillful general finds good positions everywhere for an army of 20,000 to 30,000 men—a village or a defile becoming in this case important points.

But their importance diminishes by virtue of the strength of armies. An army of 25,000 men opposed to an army of equal size is not in the same proportion as an army of 250,000 men opposed to an army of 200,000 men. Armies are in arithmetical, not in geometrical proportion. For example, an army of 25,000 men can detach only 5,000 men and still it would have great difficulty concealing it from the enemy. Besides, what can 5,000 men accomplish? The smallest fortification, the least opposition, or the slightest obstacle would stop it.

But an army of 250,000 men can make a detachment of 50,000, which is large enough to subdue a country, and the enemy would have trouble distinguishing whether he has only 200,000 men in his front instead of the 250,000 that were in line before the detachment.[5]

Composition of an Army of 80,000 Effectives

An army of 50,000 infantry, if destined to wage war in Italy, will have 10,400 cavalry, 6,000 artillery, and 1,600 belonging to the military train. The cavalry will therefore comprise nearly one fifth of the infantry, the artillery one eighth, and the military trains one thirtieth. It will form a force of 67,000 to 70,000 men present under arms on the day that the army takes the field, which assumes an effective total of 80,000 men.

The infantry will be composed of sixty battalions of six companies each: two divisions, each composed of four brigades, and one battalion for headquarters duty, for a total of twenty-six battalions; and three divisions, of three brigades each, plus one battalion for headquarters, making a total of thirty battalions. Finally there will be a reserve of four battalions.

The cavalry will be composed of sixty troops of scouts, 2,100 men; a dozen squadrons of light cavalry, 4,200 men; nine squadrons of dragoons, 3,050 men; and three squadrons of cuirassiers, 1,050 men, making a total of 10,400 men. . . .

The troops of scouts will follow their infantry battalions. The light cavalry, dragoons, and cuirassiers will be formed into four divisions, the first three of which will have one light cavalry brigade of 1,050 men and one dragoon brigade of 1,050 men, making 2,100 horses per division. The fourth division will have one brigade of cuirassiers and preferably will be attached to the reserve. The other three divisions will be united in reserve or detached to the infantry divisions, according to circumstances.

Each infantry division comprising four brigades will have three batteries of artillery; each infantry division comprising three brigades will have two batteries, and each cavalry division will have one. Five batteries of 12-pounders will march with the reserve and twelve guns will be allotted to the general park, which will comprise an artillery train for 180 guns, three for each thousand infantry and cavalry present under arms and two and one half times the effectives of these two arms. The train will comprise 104 6-pounders, forty-five howitzers, and thirty-one 12-pounders. A company of 140 men present from the military employees of engineer service [*gardes du génie*] will be placed in the train of this army.

The military train attached to this army consists of four battalions—one company of forty vehicles for each infantry division and six companies attached to the general park. The four picked companies (beasts of burden) will be detached, to wit: two to army headquarters, and a third of each of the other two companies to each infantry division. Two battalions, each of four companies, with wagons obtained by requisition, under the command of regular cadres and forming 320 wagons, will be in the rear of the army for duty with magazines and for the evacuation of hospitals.

Each infantry and cavalry division will be commanded by a major general having a colonel as chief of staff; the artillery and the cavalry will each be commanded by a lieutenant general, the corps of engineers by a major general. A major general of artillery will be director of the park, three lieutenant generals with their staffs will be under the orders of the commanding general to command the rear guard or the wings, according to his wishes. He will entrust them especially with the command of the infantry divisions whenever he unites several of them or when he unites a cavalry division.

The chief of staff will be a major general: by virtue of his position he will command all the major generals. He might not be a lieutenant general, and as soon as he is promoted to this grade he would leave the general staff. The commander in chief will be a marshal or lieutenant general. . . .

The army therefore will be composed of six infantry divisions and a reserve of four cavalry divisions: it will have nine parks of heavy baggage—six that follow the six infantry divisions, one for the reserve, one for the cavalry, and a ninth for the general park.[6]

Napoleon to General Berthier, 25 January 1800

My intention . . . is to organize an army of the reserve, the command of which will be at the disposal of the first consul. It will be divided into a right, center, and left. Each of these three large corps will be commanded by a lieutenant general who will have, in addition, one cavalry division likewise commanded by a lieutenant general.

Each of these three large corps will be divided into two divisions, each commanded by a major general and two brigadier generals, and each of the *Grand Corps* will have in addition a high-ranking artillery officer. . . .

Each corps will comprise 18,000 to 20,000 men, including the two regiments of hussars or chasseurs and sixteen guns, a dozen of which will be served by foot companies and four by the horse artillery.[7]

A Modern Army Corps

Plan of Campaign for the Army of the Rhine, 22 March 1800

The Army of the Rhine (infantry) will be divided into four *Grand Corps d'Armée.*

The First and Third Corps, each comprising three divisions:

1st division	5,000 men
2nd division	10,000 men
3rd division	5,000 men

The Second and Fourth Corps, each of four divisions:

1st division (or advance guard)	5,000 men
2nd division	10,000 men
3rd division	10,000 men
4th division	5,000 men

The first three *Grand Corps* will be designated *corps d'armée* of the Army of the Rhine; the fourth, reserve corps.

The cavalry will be divided in divisions each comprising from 2,000 to 3,000 horses.

The cavalry division attached to the reserve corps will be 3,000 men strong, two thirds of which will be chasseurs or hussars, and the rest dragoons and cavalry.

Each small division will have six guns and each large one, twelve. There will be three guns for each cavalry division.

The reserve artillery will have six 4-pounders.[8]

Napoleon to Marshal Berthier, 29 August 1805

The *Grande Armée* will be composed of seven corps:

1st Corps, composed of two divisions, each of three regiments, (or nine battalions), plus one light cavalry division of four regiments . . . commanded by Marshal Bernadotte;

2nd Corps, under the orders of General Marmont and composed of three [infantry] divisions and one light cavalry division;

3rd Corps, commanded by Marshal Davout, composed of three [infantry] divisions and one light cavalry division;

4th Corps, commanded by Marshal Soult, and composed of three [infantry] divisions and one light cavalry division;

5th Corps, commanded by Marshal Lannes, composed of three [infantry] divisions, and one light cavalry division;

6th Corps, commanded by Marshal Ney, composed of three [infantry] divisions, and one division of light cavalry;

7th Corps, commanded by Marshal Augereau, will be composed of two divisions, of nine battalions each. This corps will constitute the reserve.[9]

This is the general principle at war. A corps of 25,000 to 30,000 men can be isolated; well led, it can either fight, or avoid battle and maneuver according to circumstances without experiencing any misfortune, because it cannot be forced into battle and finally it should be able to fight for a long time. One division of 9,000 to 12,000 men can be left isolated without running into trouble for one hour. It will contain the enemy, whatever his strength, and will gain time for the army to arrive. Also it is the custom not to form an advance guard of less than 9,000 men, to have its infantry encamped well closed, and to place it more than one hour's distance from the army.[10]

War is a profession of positions, and 12,000 men are never engaged unless they choose to be. This is even more the case with 30,000 men, especially when these 30,000 are followed by other troops.[11]

VII

Strategy

The term "strategy" came into modern usage near the end of the eighteenth century. The first definitions were vague and inadequate. In 1779 the Count de Guibert used the term la stratégique *in his* Defense of the System of Modern War. *It made a difference, he asserted, whether an officer was changing front for a battalion, a regiment, a brigade, or whether he was executing the movement of larger columns involving greater time and labor and thereby limiting the span of control. No longer could the commander hope to manage separate columns personally. He could direct them only toward a given point, leaving the execution to subordinate commanders, who now had to comprehend what the Count de Guibert called "the entire art of movement or large-scale army maneuvers."*

National Military Strategy

Note on the Political and Military Position of Our Armies in Piedmont and Spain, June 1794

First Observation. If the republic had sufficient infantry to wage offensive war with its fourteen armies, it would lack the cavalry for this kind of war. If it had infantry and cavalry in sufficient numbers, it still would lack:

1. Good noncommissioned officers to lead so many troops on the offensive.
2. Suitable artillery equipment, powder, and artillery wagons.

Second Observation. It is therefore essential, when one has fourteen armies, that each wages a kind of war relative to the overall plan for the war [strategy], and to the strength and circumstances—whether topographical or political—of the opposing state.

The kind of war that each army must wage can be determined only by higher authority.

It is by these considerations above all that we are impressed with the absolute necessity that, in an immense struggle such as ours, the revolutionary government and a central authority that has a stable system devotes its full powers to every effort and thus by profound insight gives direction to courage and makes our success substantial, decisive, and less bloody.

Third Observation. The kind of war that each army must wage should therefore be determined (1) by considerations deduced from the general character of our war, (2) by the political considerations that flow from these, and (3) by military considerations.

The general principle of our war is to defend the frontiers. Austria is our most implacable enemy, therefore we must do everything possible to see that the different armies strike their blows, directly or indirectly, against this power.

If the armies along the Spanish frontier were to assume the offensive, they would undertake a war that would be separate and distinct. Austria and the German powers would not feel any effects from it, therefore it would not be compatible with the general character of our war.

Should the armies along the frontier of Piedmont assume the offensive, they would face the house of Austria to defend its Italian states and consequently this plan would be in the general character of our war.

It is the same with strategy as with the siege of a fortress: concentrate your fire against a single point, and once the wall is breached all of the rest becomes worthless and the fortress is captured. It is Germany that must be crushed; once this is accomplished Spain and Italy will fall by themselves. Therefore it is essential not to scatter our attacks but to concentrate them.

Offensive operations in Piedmont will influence Poland and encourage the Sultan of Turkey.

If we obtain great success, in the campaigns that follow we can attack Germany through Lombardy, the Ticino, and the province of Tirol, while our armies of the Rhine attack the heart. . . .

The political considerations that ought to determine the type of war for each army offer two possibilities:

1. To produce a diversion that forces the enemy to weaken himself on one of his frontiers where he retains too many troops. If our armies in Spain were to take the offensive we would obtain none of these advantages. Such a completely isolated war would not force the coalition to make any diversion. Offensive operations adopted by the armies in Piedmont would necessarily bring about a diversion along the Rhine and the northern frontiers.
2. The second possibility ought to hold out the prospect, in one or two campaigns, of overthrowing a throne and changing the government. Offensive operations by our armies in Spain cannot reasonably produce this result. Spain is a great power. The feebleness and ineptitude of the court at Madrid and the degradation of the people make it less formidable in its attacks, but the patient character of this nation, the arrogance and superstition that prevail over it, and the resources offered by its great size make Spain formidable when pushed hard on its own soil.

   Spain is a peninsula. It will have great resources in the superiority of a maritime coalition. Portugal, which does not figure in our present war, would be of great assistance to Spain. Therefore no rational mind would endeavor to take Madrid: such a plan would not be consistent with our actual position.

   Piedmont is a small state. The people there are well disposed but . . . it is small in size and lacks a distinguishable national character. It is reasonable to anticipate that in the next campaign the King eventually would be a lost sheep like his cousins. . . .

The topography of the Spanish frontier is such that, with equal forces, the advantage of the defensive is entirely on our side. The Spanish army that would be opposed to us would of course have to be much stronger in order to avoid any defeat and cause the two armies to respect each other.

When two armies are both on the defensive, the one that can most quickly concentrate several detachments to destroy an opposing force deployed in detachments manifestly would need fewer troops, and, with equal strength, would always win advantages.

The frontier of Piedmont forms a semicircle: the Army of the Alps and the Army of Italy occupy the circumference, while the King of Sardinia holds interior lines. The circumference that we occupy is filled with passes and difficult mountains, whereas the diameter held by the King of Sardinia is a fertile plain on which he can quickly reinforce one flank from the other within several days.

A defensive strategy therefore is always to the advantage of the King of Sardinia. He forces us to be twice as strong as our enemy in order to attain equal strength.

These observations are of the greatest consequence. It would be easy to demonstrate by a detailed description of the frontiers of Spain and Piedmont and an analysis of the various wars [that] . . . every time we remain on the defensive along the frontiers of Piedmont we have required many troops and have always been outnumbered in local combats.

Fourth Observation. We must therefore adopt the defensive system for the Spanish frontier and the offensive system for the Piedmont frontier:

Considerations drawn from the general spirit of our war
Political considerations
Military considerations. . . .
Attack Germany, never Spain or Italy

If we obtain great success, we must never make a change in policy by plunging into Italy, as long as Germany offers a formidable front and will not be weakened.

If national pride and revenge lure us to Rome in the next campaigns, politics and self-interest must always direct us against Vienna.

Fifth Observation. We should bring the two armies of the Alps and of Italy together and give them the same main body and esprit. Together they are sufficiently strong in infantry; it would be necessary to give them 2,000 cavalry and restore the departments which have been taken away from them, add some new ones, and give them a portion of the wagon transport now with the Army of the Pyrenees—generally everything that will no longer be needed by that army because of the defensive strategy that it would adopt.

The armies of the Alps and of Italy have sufficient artillery; they lack only a few particular small stores that have already been requested from the commissions. They need especially powder, harness, and horses. . . .

In the next campaign this army should be increased progressively to enable it to accomplish everything that it is capable of doing

Sixth Observation. The present campaign moves forward, but if the armies of Piedmont are able to procure winter quarters in enemy territory and force the Emperor of Austria to make a powerful diversion, they will have achieved their objective for this campaign, established the foundation for following campaigns, and dealt an essential blow to the house of Austria in Germany.[1]

The Strategic Situation

Napoleon to the Executive Directory, 1 February 1798

In the existing situation in Europe, prudence compels us to be prepared to wage war on our various frontiers . . . at the first indication from other powers.

In Italy we have 16,000 French and 5,000 Poles—21,000 men against the King of Naples, which, in addition to 2,000 troops that the government has ordered to prepare at Toulon for a landing, are sufficient so that we have nothing to fear from this monarch.

We have in Italy, against the [Austrian] Emperor, 21,000 men, which, added to the 4,000 that the government is going to place at the disposal of this army, amounts to 25,000 men. We could count on nearly 10,000 poor Cisalpine troops, in all a total of 35,000 men, which is an extremely small number to man the fortresses and form a corps of observation, compared with the 80,000 men that the Emperor has on this frontier.

But all of the forces of the republic can assemble in Germany to rescue Italy very quickly and prevent the fortresses from being taken.

It would be very easy for us to bring the Army of Mayence up to 80,000 or 90,000 men and to have 40,000 to 50,000 on Lake Constance, reinforced by a determined number of Swiss. These two armies would unite very quickly to attack the House of Austria in the heart of its hereditary estates.

If we were to wage war against the King of Prussia, the Army of Mayence and that of Holland would very quickly attack in the Bishopric of Münster and enter Hanover.

But, in any case, it is essential . . . not to lose precious time, for should war occur, those who strike the first blows . . . will have, by their position, great advantages.[2]

The Egyptian Campaign

Napoleon to the Executive Directory, 7 October 1798

The Ottoman government has named Djezzar, Pasha of Acre, commander in chief of all Syria. He has not responded to any overture that I have made him. Everywhere our consuls are in custody, and throughout the Ottoman Empire everything reverberates with the sound of war. . . .

This country is surrounded by Arab forces, ferocious, numerous, and brave. All of the tribes united make a total of 12,000 cavalry and 50,000 infantry. The population of the interior is composed of different elements, all accustomed to being defeated or winning, being tyrants or being oppressed. The soil is the most beautiful on earth, and its location likewise interesting and decisive for India. The European power that controls Egypt will, in the long run, control India. . . . It could be advantageous for the republic to make the conquest of Egypt pave the way for a glorious peace with England. . . .

If the Emperor of Constantinople makes war on us and the Holy Roman Emperor and the Russian Emperor are undecided, we could be attacked at sea by the English and the Turks, and by land in the interior.

Spain therefore betrays us since it leaves the English absolute master of the Mediterranean.[3]

The Marengo Campaign

Napoleon to General Moreau, Commander in Chief of the Army of the Rhine, 22 March 1800

The consuls of the republic have decreed . . . after having considered the position of our troops in Switzerland, on the Rhine, in Italy, and the formation of the army of the reserve at Dijon, the following plan of operations:

1. That it is necessary to begin the campaign no later than between 10 and 20 April.
2. That the actual Army of the Rhine will be divided into army corps and a reserve corps. . . .
3. From 10 to 20 April you will cross the Rhine with your army corps, profiting from the advantages that the occupation of Switzerland offers you to outflank the Black Forest and nullify the preparations that the enemy could have made to dispute the gorges.
4. The reserve corps will be especially charged with guarding Switzerland. Its advance guard, some 5,000 to 6,000 strong, will occupy the Saint-Gotthard. . . .
5. The objective of your movement into Germany with your army corps must be to push the enemy into Bavaria in such a way as to intercept his direct communication with Milan by Lake Constance and the Grisons.

6. As soon as this objective is accomplished and we can be assured that in any event the main enemy army, even assuming that it might force you to fall back, will not be able to reconquer the territory that it will have lost in ten or twelve days' time, the intention of the consuls is to have Switzerland defended by the last divisions of the army of reserve, composed of less experienced troops than the corps that comprises your reserve, and to detach your reserve with the elite of the army of reserve at Dijon to invade Switzerland by the Saint-Gotthard and the Simplon and bring about the junction with the Army of Italy in the plains of Lombardy.[4]

Napoleon to General Masséna, Commander in Chief of the Army of Italy, 9 April 1800

In their operations the Army of the Rhine under General in Chief Moreau, and the army of the reserve under the orders of General Berthier now assembling at Dijon, must communicate with each other and execute simultaneously and with great harmony.

The Army of the Rhine will take the field first, which will occur from the 10th to the 20th of April. It will be divided into two parts: one, about 100,000 strong, under the immediate command of General Moreau, will cross the Rhine, enter Swabia, and advance by the side of Bavaria until it can intercept, by its position, the communication of Germany with Milan by the route from Feldkirch, Coire, and the Italian bailliages of Switzerland.

The other corps of the Army of the Rhine, forming its right flank, will be about 25,000 men under the immediate orders of General Lecourbe. Its mission is first to occupy Switzerland in order to secure the right flank of the corps that is to enter Swabia, to facilitate this invasion, and to keep the enemy out of Switzerland by preventing them from penetrating by way of Rheineck, Feldkirch, the Grisons, the Saint-Gotthard pass, or the Simplon. Once this initial mission is fulfilled and General Moreau has made his way a dozen or fifteen marches from these Rhine crossings, General Lecourbe will pass with his corps under the orders of General Berthier, cross the Saint-Gotthard pass, and enter into Italy. At the same time one portion of the army of the reserve will . . . also penetrate into Italy either by the Simplon or the Saint-Gotthard, while the rest of this army will take the place of the corps commanded by General Lecourbe in Switzerland.

It is at this precise moment . . . when the troops commanded by General Berthier will have entered Italy, that you must combine your movements with his in order to attract the attention of the enemy, compel him to divide his forces, and bring about your junction with the corps that will have penetrated into Italy. Until then you will maintain the defensive. The mountains that cover you, by making the enemy cavalry and artillery inactive, will assure your superiority in this strategy ["system of war"], that is to say, the certainty of maintaining yourself in your positions, which, up to this point, must be your true and only objective. .

Any offensive on your part would be dangerous before this point because, when your army moves into the plains it would restore to action those enemy forces that are paralyzed by the nature of the mountainous country you now occupy. It would be impossible to send you enough help directly to give you a decided superiority. It is from Switzerland that this help would arrive, by attacking the rear of the enemy. Once your junction is accomplished, this superiority will be decided; then the offensive will be resumed, the fortresses of Piedmont and Milan will be seized or blockaded, and the French army will emerge by its own courage from the shocking scarcities we suffer, and which we cannot effectually remedy.

If special circumstances cause the columns penetrating into Italy, either by the Saint-Gotthard and the Simplon or by one of these two passes, to reunite, they will probably total about 65,000 men, comprising General Lecourbe's column of 25,000 and General Berthier's 40,000, in which he will find nearly 6,000 cavalry and 2,000 artillery.

To debouch into Italy you will assemble the forces at your disposal in the rear as far as the Var; you will gather from those scattered from the Var to Mount Cenis all men whom you judge fit and prudent to reinforce yourself, and those who shall remain from Mount Cenis as far as Valais will form a special corps placed at the disposition of General Berthier to facilitate his movement. . . .

When your operations will have advanced to this point I will transmit further instructions . . . for the achievement of the campaign.

You know very well . . . the importance of the most profound secrecy in such circumstances. . . . You will employ all the demonstrations and appearances of movement that you judge convenient to deceive the enemy about the real strategical objective and persuade him that he will first be attacked by you. Therefore exaggerate your forces and announce immense and near reinforcements approaching from the interior. Finally, you will mislead the enemy, insofar as it is possible, about the true points of attack, which are the Saint-Gotthard and the Simplon.[5]

The first consul ordered General Moreau to take the offensive and enter Germany in order to stop the movement of the Austrian Army of Italy, which had already arrived at Genoa. The entire Army of the Rhine was to unite in Switzerland and cross the Rhine to the height of Schaffhausen, the movement from the left of the army to its right being screened by the Rhine, and elsewhere being prepared well in advance so that the enemy would have no knowledge of it. By throwing four bridges simultaneously at the hill of Schaffhausen the entire French army would cross in twenty-four hours, reach Stockach and overthrow the enemy's left, taking from the rear all Austrian fortresses between the right bank of the Rhine and the defiles of the Black Forest. In six or seven days after opening the campaign the army would be in front of Ulm. Those Austrian units that could escape would fall back into Bohemia. Thus the first movement of the campaign would result in separating the Austrian army from Ulm, Philippsburg, and Ingolstadt and giving our own forces possession of Württemberg, all of Swabia and Bavaria. This operational plan must give rise to more or less decisive events, depending upon the chances of fortune and the audacity and rapidity of the movements of the French general.

General Moreau was incapable of executing or even comprehending such a movement. He sent General Dessolles to Paris to present another plan to the minister of war. Following the practice of the campaigns of 1796 and 1797, he proposed to cross the Rhine at Mayence, Strasbourg, and Basle. Strongly opposed to this plan, I considered for a moment placing myself at the head of this army, calculating that it would be under the walls of Vienna before the Austrian Army of Italy could be in front of Nice. But the internal agitation of the republic worked against my leaving the capital and . . . being away for so long a time. Instead Moreau's plan was modified and he was authorized to carry out a compromise plan. . . . He was especially told to have only a single line of operations. Moreover, in the execution this latter plan appeared too bold for him and he made some changes.[6]

The Ulm Campaign, 1805

Marshal Berthier, Chief of Staff, to General Gouvion Saint-Cyr, 2 September 1805. By Order of the Emperor.

I have no faith in waiting until the last moment to inform you of the plan of campaign adopted by the Emperor: it is advantageous that you be instructed fifteen days in advance in order that you can make all of your preparations in the most profound secrecy, so that when I transmit the Emperor's orders to commence hostilities you will be prepared to play the important role that His Majesty, in his vast plans from the Baltic as far as Naples, has entrusted to you.

You will have 20,000 men—either French, Polish, Swiss, or Italian—when hostilities begin. This force, sufficient to capture Naples, drive away the court, and dispel and destroy the Neapolitan army, would no longer suffice if 12,000 Russians and 6,000 English, from Corfu and Malta, had time to plan together with the Neapolitan army.

It is essential that you take the initiative in these movements. You must therefore gain time, modify your projects drastically, and, right up to the moment when your operations begin, do nothing that would cause uneasiness with the King of Naples.

The intention of the Emperor is that you will enter Naples at the same time that he crosses the Rhine, which would occur in the first part of *vendémiaire*. By then you will have forestalled the plans of the Russians and the English; you will be master of Naples before they have learned that hostilities have even commenced. You will have broken up the Neapolitan army and you will have had time to seize the forts.

You will establish at Naples a regency in the form of a provisional government, and you will do whatever is convenient to stroke the views of those who are against the court.

Your subsequent conduct will depend on how the Russians and the English react. They may reunite everybody in Sicily to await new help and plan an invasion to retake Naples, in which case the months will pass and you will have a part of the winter to arm, if it is possible, the party that supports your side and to await the result of the great events in Germany.

Alternatively, if 10,000 Russians attempt to disembark at Taranto, you would be strong enough to march against them before they could re-form and mount their artillery and cavalry. Do not spare yourself; and if, by some combinations that might occur, the enemy forces were such that you would be compelled to evacuate Naples and the southern portion of the kingdom, you could dispute the terrain and make your retreat slowly.

When you reach Pescara, you will leave Major General Reynier to command the fortress there, with a strong garrison and abundant stock for artillery, provisions, etc., and you will continue your retreat on Parma or Tuscany, according to whatever events may have transpired in upper Italy.

Therefore you can consider your plans from two points of view. As opposition to the Neapolitan army your operations are of little use as general operations; but, considered from the point of view of an army of observation opposing a coalition, you prevent or delay considerably their junction with the Austrian Army of the Adige.

The great blows will be struck in Germany, where the Emperor will go in person, and even if the operations of the Army of Italy are not successful, this must not influence your efforts . . . because any success the enemy could obtain would only be of short duration. . . . If the Emperor's operations are crowned with the success that we have a right to expect, their first result will be to extricate the Army of Italy and send you the support you would need to throw the coalition forces into the sea, recapture all of the country that you will have lost, and even to threaten Sicily.

In the final analysis, you must begin the armament and supply of Pescara without delay, placing there all the depots of your army. . . . It is precisely to this point that help will be directed and it is your center of operations. This fortress must be held several months, even if you are forced to evacuate the surrounding country, thus giving the Emperor time to complete his plan. . . .

This letter is the principal instruction for your plan of campaign, and if unforeseen events should occur, you will be guided in your conduct by the spirit of this instruction.[7]

Napoleon to Joseph, 31 December 1805

My intention is to conquer the Kingdom of Naples. Marshal Masséna and General Saint-Cyr are now marching on that kingdom with two army corps. I have named you my lieutenant commander in chief of the Army of Naples. . . . You will find at army headquarters your instructions and the decrees relating to your mission.[8]

Napoleon to Joseph, 12 January 1806

I calculate that after several days' rest you will have nearly 40,000 men, which you can divide into three corps. Marshal Masséna will have the strongest, General Saint-Cyr the second, and General Reynier the smallest, consisting of 6,000 good troops, in reserve. Attach yourself to General Reynier: he is aloof, but of the three he is the most capable of making a good campaign plan and providing sound advice. In your position the art is to make each of the three believe that he shares your confidence. . . .

Your great task is to keep all your forces together and to reach Naples as quickly as possible with your entire command. . . . Never hold a council of war, but listen to the views of each in private. . . . Prince Eugene, who commands in the Kingdom of Italy, will hold a reserve ready to meet any unexpected event.

You should establish your line of communication, that is to say, your route of posts and halting places at the end of each day's march, by Tuscany and not by Ancona and the Abruzzi, for I want you to move against Naples by way of Rome. . . .

Keep your forces united.[9]

Napoleon to Joseph, 19 January 1806

My intention is that you enter the Kingdom of Naples in the first days of February and that I be notified, during the course of the month, that my eagles fly over this capital. . . .

I repeat: do not divide your forces. Let your entire army pass the Apennines and your three corps march against Naples, positioned in such a way that they can be united on the same battlefield in a single day. Leave a general officer and some depots, stores, and artillery men at Ancona to defend the fortress. . . . Once Naples is taken, the outlying parts of the kingdom will fall by themselves. The enemy forces in Abruzzi will be taken in the rear, and you will send one division to Taranto and another near Sicily to complete the conquest of the kingdom. . . .

The country must supply you with provisions, clothes, remounts, and everything necessary for your army so that it will not cost me a sou.[10]

Napoleon to Joseph, 7 February 1808

I wrote to you on 24 January about the Sicilian operation. I assume that you have made the necessary preparations. Here is the news that I have received this morning.

Admiral Ganteaume informs me that on 3 February, from the roadstead at Toulon, my squadron from Rochefort has been sighted at Villefranche at 10:00 A.M., that consequently he ordered up anchor to go to reconnoiter and that he probably would move to Corfu to give chase to the English fleet and aid in the passage of all the vessels from Brindisi and Otrante to Corfu, and endeavor to take some enemy ships.

You know how important it is that you keep the most profound secrecy, and that in the meantime you send without delay two trustworthy and intelligent officers, one to Otrante and Brindisi and the other to Taranto. Those that you send to Otrante and Brindisi must see to it that all convoys found in these ports are ready to hoist sail, so that Corfu is abundantly provisioned.

Corfu is so important to me that its loss would be a fatal blow to my plans. The Adriatic would be closed and your kingdom [Spain] would have on its left flank a port where the enemy could recruit Albanians and other troops to attack you. On the other side they would endeavor to have great influence in Albania. Therefore I count on your zeal that nothing is forgotten, and to benefit from this unique circumstance to shelter Corfu in any event. . . .

My intention is that you embark another French battalion without delay . . . which would give you a total of 7,500 men. Then the English could not descend on it and I will always be master of this island. . . .

This plan is based upon the principle that you are master of Scilla, the most important port in the world. If you are not master of Scilla, everything would be impossible and Sicily would be lost as a result of your error.[11]

Notes on the Actual Position of the Army in Spain, 21 July 1808[12]

1. The battle of Medina de Río Seco has placed the affairs of the army in the best situation. Marshal Bessières no longer gives cause for any anxiety, and all concerns must be directed toward General Dupont.
2. In the actual state of affairs, the French army occupies the center and the enemy a large number of points on the circumference.
3. In a war of this nature we must be composed, patient, and calculating. We must not exhaust the troops in needless marches and countermarches. We must not assume that when we have made one false march of three or four days that we could make up for it by one countermarch: this is usually committing two mistakes instead of one.

4. All operations of the army so far have succeeded—as much as they deserve to succeed—up to this hour. General Dupont has held his ground on the other side of the mountains and in the basins of Andalusia. Three times he has defeated the insurgents.
5. Marshal Moncey has defeated the insurgents in Valencia. He has not been able to take the city, which is not unusual. Perhaps it would have been desirable if he could have encamped one day in the city, as General Dupont has done; but after all, whether it would be for one day or five, as at San Clemente, the difference is not very great.

In Aragón we have defeated the enemy at all points and under all circumstances and produced discouragement everywhere. Saragossa has not been taken. Today it is surrounded, and a city of 40,000 to 50,000 population defended by a popular movement can be taken only with time and patience. Histories of wars are filled with too many illustrious catastrophes for us to hasten to get into a scrape in the narrow city streets. One example would be Buenos Aires and the 12,000 elite English troops who perished there.[13]

Thus the position of the army is good, With Marshal Moncey being at San Clemente or its environs and Generals Gobert and Vedel reunited with General Dupont in Andalusia, it would be a mistake—unless for incidents and an immediate need to strike some other point with these troops—to concentrate all troops too close to Madrid. The uncertainty of the results of Marshal Bessières and the twenty-five percent chance working against him might cause one to halt the march of all the troops that are far from the capital, thus enabling the columns to be recalled to Madrid, if Marshal Bessières were defeated, in time to reach this city before the enemy. But this would be a mistake if we had caused these columns to fall back and acted as though Marshal Bessières had been defeated when, several days earlier, he operated as though the Army of Galicia did not exist. Five hundred cavalry and 1,800 infantry directed against Valladolid were all that he needed.

Had this column departed three days earlier, it would

have arrived there on the 17th. Marshal Bessières would have been the victor and in this circumstance the odds were sixty-five to twenty-five in his favor. But the fatigue that this produced in the army and the retrograde movements that had been needlessly ordered after that—even with Marshal Bessières defeated we had eight to ten days in which to reunite the army—caused a moral and physical hardship. One must hope that news of his victory, arriving in time, will have caused the general staff even to stop all movement toward Madrid and that each column will find itself nearer the point where it should be.

6. Given the actual state of affairs, the most important of all is General Dupont: he must be sent the remainder of Gobert's division and use other troops to maintain lines of communication. The head of Marshal Moncey's division must be kept in San Clemente as a constant threat to the province of Valencia. If Marshal Bessières has defeated the Army of Galicia without effort and with light casualties, and if he has fewer than 8,000 men engaged, there is no doubt that General Dupont, with 20,000, will succeed in overthrowing the force in his front.
7. General Rey's brigade restores to the army more than it has lost by the detachment which has been made toward Valladolid. All human probabilities are that Marshal Bessières no longer needs any reinforcement in order to be master of all of Castile and the Kingdom of León. Only when we receive news of what he will have accomplished at Benavente and León should we determine if he needs to attack Galicia.
8. General Verdier, in Aragón, has invested Saragossa. The 14th and 44th regiments of the line depart tomorrow to go there. French detachments are going as far as halfway on the road from Lérida, Barbastro, and Jaca. In ten days all of the artillery will have arrived. This fine and good brigade of troops of the line brings the army of General Verdier to nearly 15,000 men. It is likely that Saragossa will soon fall and that two thirds of these 15,000 men will become available.
9. Thus the corps of Marshal Bessières has taken the offensive. Since his victory he has been reinforced by the brigade of

Lefebvre and the Gaulic brigade. He is therefore able to maintain the offensive.

General Verdier's corps, in Aragón, has defeated the insurgents everywhere and has invested the city with much smaller forces. He has just been considerably reinforced, so he can devote increased activity to siege operations and maintain his offensive activity along both banks of the Ebro.

The corps from Catalonia has acted in isolation, with Barcelona for its base. The junction with General Reille will be made today or tomorrow.

That accounts for the three army corps located on the coast of France.

10. The communication of Madrid with France is important from every point of view: it is therefore necessary that the columns which have just been organized at Burgos and Vitoria and will be daily reinforced and augmented are left at these stations. . . . These columns are nearly all composed of third battalions and conscripts, but they have good cadres. Fifteen to twenty days of duty at Burgos and Vitoria will get them nearly to the *School of the Battalion* in their drill manual. It would be a great mistake to call up these troops to reinforce the main cadres too soon. We must wait until we have been able to replace them at Vitoria and Burgos with new troops.

11. There is nothing to fear, therefore, from the direction of Marshal Bessières, nor in the north of Castile or the Kingdom of León.

There is nothing to fear in Aragón: Saragossa will fall one day sooner or a day later.

There is nothing to fear in Catalonia.

There is nothing to fear for the communications from Burgos to Bayonne, thanks to the two columns that are organized in these cities and which will be reinforced.

If anything should happen in Biscayes, the force assembled at Bayonne, forming a reserve, would be sufficient to put everything in order.

If some event should occur at Burgos too important for the mobile column at Burgos to handle, Marshal Bessières will not be so far away that he could not make a detachment.

General Monthion has the supervision of all of Biscayes. General Bonnet at Burgos is charged with maintaining communication from Vitoria with Marshal Bessières and with Madrid. It is necessary that these two generals correspond with each other every day and with General Drouet, who remains in reserve at Bayonne, as well as with General Verdier at Saragossa and General d'Agoult at Pampeluna. They must also maintain daily correspondence with General Drouet at Bayonne and with Madrid. . . . A courier leaving Madrid could go by way of Vitoria, Tolosa, and Pampeluna previous to Saragossa.

The only point important today, therefore, is that of General Dupont. Should the enemy ever succeed in getting hold of the defiles of the Sierra Morena it would be difficult to dislodge him. It would therefore be necssary to reinforce General Dupont so that he would have 25,000 men, including what he would need to guard the mountain passes and a portion of the road from la Manche. He will be able to dispose of his troops in such a way that the day when he desires to attack, the brigade of 2,000 or 3,000 men designated to guard the mountains could reach General Dupont's camp by forced marches, and would be successively replaced by columns that would be in the rear, so that General Dupont would have more than 23,000 men to take position in line for the day of battle.

Once we have defeated the enemy, a portion of the troops of the line will be dispersed and, depending upon whether the victory is more or less decided, we would have the movement of other troops under General Dupont continued.

12. With the capture of Saragossa General Dupont will have at his disposal the troops either to reinforce the army of Catalonia, or to march against Valencia in concert with Marshal Moncey, or to reinforce Marshal Bessières and march into Galicia if, after the victory that he has already won and that which he will win at León, he does not consider himself strong enough to do so from the very first.

13. It should be important to select two intermediate points between Andújar and Madrid where we could leave permanent

garrisons, a commandant, an ammunition depot, magazines for bread ovens, flour, and a hospital so that 300 or 400 men can defend the magazines and the hospital against any insurrection.

It is difficult to believe that there is no such château . . . capable of being intrenched promptly that would be appropriate for this. It is the only way that we can shorten the line of communications and be sure of having an army bakery and a resting place every three or four full marches. . . .

Today the only place that is threatened, where we must promptly gain success, is with General Dupont. With 25,000 men, including cavalry and artillery, he has more than enough to get great results. As a rule, with 21,000 men present on the battlefield, he can boldly assume the offensive; he will not be defeated, and he will have odds of better than four to one in his favor.[14]

VIII

Fortification

"It is evident that without fortifications a place cannot be considered secure unless held by considerably greater numbers than the enemy can bring to assail it. No less an authority than Napoleon says that, aided by fortifications, 50,000 men and 3,000 artillery can defend a capital against 300,000 men, and he asserts the necessity of fortifying all national capitals."

—*Brig. Gen. John G. Barnard, 22 January 1862*

It is necessary to determine the perception on the utility of fortified cities. There are fortified cities that defend a gorge and which, by that fact alone, have a fixed character. There are fortified cities that can contain large garrisons and resist for a long time, providing an inferior army has the means of being reinforced, reorganizing itself, and attempting new risks. In the first instance a fort or small town could be mentioned; in the second, a large fortified city, where one must spare neither money nor fortified works, is appropriate.

In addition to these two cases there is a third—the fortification of an entire frontier. Thus the frontier from Dunkerque to Maubeuge presents a large number of fortified towns of different sizes and importance, placed *en échiquier* in three lines so that it is physically impossible to pass on without having captured several of them. In this case a small fortified town has for its objective to support the flooding that runs from one city to the next, or to create a bottleneck. Then there is established, in the midst of all these fortified cities, a different kind of war. The capture of a convoy or the surprise of a magazine gives the advantage to a greatly inferior army without measuring swords or running any risk of having a siege raised or an operation fail. This is, in brief, the affair of Denain, a combat of little importance in itself, but one that nevertheless very clearly saved France from the greatest catastrophes.[1]

Fortified towns are useful for defensive as well as offensive war. While they cannot in themselves take the place of an army, they constitute the only means one has to delay, check, weaken, or harass an enemy conquerer. . . . Garrisons of fortified cities should be taken from the local population and not from active armies: regiments of provincial militia have this destination. It is the most lofty prerogative of the National Guard.

Perhaps Vauban's system is defective, but it remains the best that has been offered. He would prefer to centralize, unite, gather his forces, his artillery, and his war machines than to scatter them.[2]

Have the frontier fortresses of Flanders been useful or detrimental? . . . To defend one's capital, should an army cover it by retreating into it? Should it occupy an intrenched camp, supported by a fortified town, or should it maneuver freely so as not to allow itself to be driven into a corner, either in the capital or in a fortress?

The defense system of the frontier of Flanders in large measure has been conceived by Vauban, but this engineer was forced to utilize fortresses already in existence. He had some new ones constructed to cover the sluices, extend inundations, or to block the important gaps between large forests or mountains. . . . Fifty thousand men of the National Guard of the interior suffice to make these secure from a sudden attack and beyond the threat of incendiary batteries. Lille, Valenciennes, and Charlemont as well as the intrenched camps of Maubeuge and Cambrai could provide such refuge to armies.

Vauban has organized entire districts into intrenched camps covered by streams, inundations, fortified towns, and forests, but he never contended that the fortified cities alone could close the frontier. He intended that this frontier, thus fortified, would provide protection for an inferior army against a superior one, that it would give him a field of operations favorable for maintaining his army and preventing the enemy army from advancing; that it would offer occasions for attacking with advantage; and, finally, that it would provide the means for gaining time to enable help to arrive.

During the reverses of Louis XIV this system of fortified towns saved the capital. Prince Eugene of Savoy lost an entire campaign season in order to take Lille. The siege of Landrecies offered Villars the chance to change his fortune. A hundred years later, in 1793, during the treason of Dumouriez, the fortified towns of Flanders saved Paris.[3] The enemy coalition lost an entire campaign before taking Condé, Valenciennes, Le Quesnoy, and Landrecies. This line of fortresses was equally useful in 1814. The allies violated Swiss territory and became entangled in the defiles of Jura trying to avoid the fortresses, and in this outflanking movement they were forced to commit a large number of troops than the total size of the French garrisons. . . .

When I crossed the Marne and maneuvered against the rear of the enemy army, the frontier fortresses would have played a significant role had treason not opened the gates of Paris. . . . They would likewise have been of great utility in 1815, for the Anglo-Prussian armies would not have dared cross the Somme before the arrival of the Austro-Russian armies on the Marne were it not for the insurrection of the French chambers. Those fortresses that remained faithful had an influence upon the conditions in the treaties and the conduct of the enemy monarchs in 1814 and 1815.[4]

In the last century the question was raised whether fortifications were of any utility. It is the sovereigns who have judged them useless and who would consequently have dismantled their fortresses. As for me, I would reverse the question and ask if it is possible to plan war without them? The answer must be no. Without fortified depots it is impossible to establish good plans of campaign, and without fortified towns—which I call field depots [*places de campagne*]—in other words fortifications safe even from hussars and detachments, one cannot wage offensive war. Also several generals who in their wisdom did not desire fortified towns, ultimately concluded that it is not possible to wage a war of invasion.

But how many fortified towns are necessary? On this issue one convinces himself that the principle is the same for fortified towns as for the placement of troops. Do you assume you can defend an entire frontier by a cordon? You are weak everywhere, for in the final analysis everything that is human has limits—artillery, money, good officers, and good generals: these are not infinite, and if you are forced to scatter your resources everywhere you will not be strong anywhere.[5]

Napoleon to General Dejean, 3 September 1806

Enclosed you will find the report of the director of engineers in Dalmatia. I have asked him how Austria could attack Dalmatia, but he does not understand this question. I appreciate that in order to respond he would have me survey the frontier of Dalmatia and Austria, indicate the points where the Austrian army could assemble its magazines in Croatia, the direction that it would give to its columns to penetrate into Dalmatia, and finally the defensive positions in Dalmatia on the side toward Austria.

I have informed him that I intend Zara to be considered as the center of the defense of all Dalmatia. He did not understand, however, what I mean by this expression. He believes that I want all of the troops assembled at Zara and that I thought that the point of defense should emanate from this fortress, whether Dalmatia was attacked by Austria or the attacks were to come from the Turkish frontier, or whether they might come from a seaborne landing. . . .

Dalmatia can be attacked by sea and its ports and harbors need batteries to defend them. There are many islands that are important. Several forts exist near the large towns and the main ports could also be important, but this importance is secondary.

Dalmatia, on the land side, shares a lengthy frontier with Austria and Turkey. Several forts exist that defend the defiles or mountain passages. These can be useful, but their usefulness is secondary.

Both are fieldworks, although permanent fortifications, and I label them such because they can serve to shelter a detachment or battalion against either a landing or an invasion while the French army is superior in Dalmatia, however inferior it may find itself for the moment at the point of the invasion landing. . . . These forts . . . can serve and aid in the movements and the defensive maneuvers of the French army, but they will fall the moment the enemy's superiority over the French army is clearly established.

There is no way to prevent an army two or three times the size of the forces I would have in Dalmatia from making good its landing at any point along eighty leagues of coastline and quickly obtaining a decided advantage over my army, if its constitution is proportionate to its numbers.

It is likewise impossible to prevent a stronger army that would debouch by the Austrian or Turkish border from gaining advantages over my army in Dalmatia.

But is it necessary for the 6,000, 8,000, or 12,000 men, which the general political situation allows me to maintain in Dalmatia, to be destroyed and without resources after several combats? Must my munitions, hospitals, and magazines, scattered at random, fall and become the enemy's prize as soon as he acquires superiority in the field over my army of Dalmatia?

No! This is precisely the situation that I must anticipate and avoid. I can accomplish it only through the establishment of a great fortress, a fortified depot that functions as a redoubt for the entire defense of Dalmatia, which would contain all of my hospitals, magazines, and establishments, where all of my troops in Dalmatia come to re-form and rally, either to shut themselves up in the fortress or else to return to the field, depending upon the nature of events and the strength of the enemy army.

I consider this fortified town to be the central fortress. As long as it exists, my troops might lose battles but they will not suffer more than the ordinary losses of war. As long as it exists the troops themselves, after recovering their breath and rest, can seize the victory or at least offer me the comparable advantages, tying up three times the number of enemy troops in besieging this fortress, thus giving me three or four months' time to march to their relief. For as long as the fortress is not captured the fate of the province remains undecided and the immense matériel attached to the defense of such a large province is not lost.

Thus all of the forts located at mountain defiles or intended for the protection of the different islands and ports are of secondary utility. My intention is that we work only to improve or augment these fortifications, so that I know that the details of the works of the principal fortress have reached a sufficient degree of strength, and that my munitions of war, hospitals, clothing magazines, and storehouses are centralized in my fortified depot, which must provide whatever is necessary for the defense of the localities, but in such a way that little time at all is needed to fall back to this fortress. . . .

Once a central fortress exists, all of the campaign plans of my generals should be based upon it. If a larger army should land at any point whatever, the concern of the generals should be to direct all operations in such a way that their retreat to the central fortress is always assured.

If an army should attack the Turkish or Austrian frontier the same consideration must direct all operations of the French generals. Unable to defend the entire province, they must defend the province from the central fortress. All magazines of the army will be concentrated there, all kinds of lavish defenses will exist there, and a constant goal will be given to the operations of the generals. Everything becomes simple, easy, and resolved; nothing is vague when one establishes, of long standing and by superior authority, the central point of a country. We know how much security . . . this central point can provide and the assurance it offers the individual soldier comprising the army. The interest of self-preservation acts sufficiently on each man so that he feels isolated and vulnerable. On one coast the sea covers with enemy ships, on the other, the mountains of the Bosnian barbarians, and on a third side the mountains next to Croatia, nearly unnegotiable in a retreat, especially when the country is considered enemy territory. Too much uneasiness exists in the army if, in such a position, it does not have a simple and predetermined plan. . . . When, after several months' campaigning, one can always as a last resource take refuge in a fortified city that is abundantly provisioned, he has more than the guarantee of life: he has the guarantee of honor.[6]

IX

The Army in the Field

"A general should be capable of making all the resources of the invaded country contribute to the success of his enterprise."

—Lt. Gen. Antoine-Henri, Baron de Jomini

The direction of military affairs is only half of a general's work. One of the most important things is to establish and secure one's line of operation,[1] by which I mean your line of posts and halting places[2] where the hospitals, help for the sick, munitions of war, and provisions are located and where the army can reorganize, make good its losses, and with a couple of days' rest recover its morale, which is sometimes lost by an unexpected accident. One dare not lose his line of operation. According to the laws of war, the general who loses his line of operation deserves death.[3]

Every five or six marches you must have a fortified city or intrenched position along the line of operation where you can assemble the magazines for victuals and military supplies, organize convoys, and which you can make the center of maneuver, a pivot mark that shortens the line of operation.

Ulm is the first natural pivot for the invasion of Germany. This fortress, situated on the Danube, provides facilities to the army that controls it for maneuvering along both banks. It is the only place to contain the large depots on the largest river in Europe, the river that washes the walls of Ingolstadt, Ratisbon, Passau, and Vienna. From the direction of France this fortress stands at the outlet of the Black Mountains.

As we advance into enemy territory, new fortified cities to serve as depots will be designated. . . . Since these depots are protected by fortifications, whatever is left behind in them is not endangered. Regimental registers, papers, the magazines, and everything else of this nature, plus everything that the soldier does not carry in his knapsack or the officer in his valise, must remain in these depots. . . .

During the march of the army all men unfit to follow their units will be sent to the various depots.[4] All malingerers and tired men in need of rest will be left at these depots. Each army corps will leave behind one field officer to command these men, and when they are rested and in condition to be put on the road the depot commander will . . . form them into "marching battalions" to be sent forward to the army. . . . All wounded horses belonging to the cavalry, artillery, and the military train will be sent immediately to the nearest cavalry depot.[5] Every kind of impedimenta will be directed to the . . . depots so that the army is mobile and light, and encumbered as little as possible.[6]

In my first Italian campaign in 1796 I set out from Savona, which served as my fortified depot, crossed the mountains . . . where the Alps end and the Apennines begin, drove a wedge between the Austrian and Sardinian armies, and captured Cherasco, a fortress at the confluence of the Tanaro and the Stura, twenty leagues from Savona, and established my magazines there. I made the King of Sardinia surrender the fortified city of Tortona, located twenty leagues east of Cherasco in the direction of Milan. Establishing myself there, I then crossed the Po at Plaisance, seized Pizzighettone, a fortified place on the Adda twenty-five leagues from Tortona, moved on the Mincio, seized Peschiera, thirty leagues from Pizzighettone, and then took the line of the Adige, occupying the wall and the fort of Verona on the left bank, which secured me the three stone bridges, at Porto-Legnago, which gave me another bridge over this river.

I remained at this position until the capture of Mantua, which I had ordered invested and besieged. From my camp near Verona, at Chambéry, the first depot this side of the French frontier, I had four fortified cities in echelon containing my hospitals and magazines and requiring only 4,000 men to garrison. The convalescents and conscripts were sufficient. Thus I had, along this line of 100 leagues, one fortified depot every four marches. After the capture of Mantua, when I moved into the Papal States, Ferrara served as my fortified depot on the Po, and Ancona, seven or eight marches farther, my second fort at the foot of the Apennines.

In the 1797 campaign I crossed the Piave and the Tagliamento, fortified Palmanova and Osoppo, some eight marches from Mantua, crossed the Julian Alps, repaired the old fortifications of Klagenfurt, five marches from Osoppo, and took position on the Soemmering. There I found myself forty-five leagues from Mantua: on this line of operation I had three fortified cities in echelon and one supporting point every five or six marches.

In 1798 I began my operations in the Orient with the capture of Alexandria, a large city which I fortified and made the hub of my magazines and headquarters. Marching to Cairo I had a fort established at El-Rahmânyeh, on the Nile, twenty leagues from Alexandria and thirty from Cairo. At Cairo I had a citadel and several forts constructed, and erected another one thirty leagues from the capital at Sâlheyeh, at the entrance to the desert on the road to Gaza. The army, encamped in this village, found itself fifteen marching days from Alexandria, but it had three fortified bases along this line of operation.

During the campaign of 1799 I crossed eighty leagues of desert, besieged Saint-Jean-d'Acre and pushed my corps of observation to the Jordan, 250 leagues from Alexandria, my main depot. But I had a fort built at Oatyeh, in the desert, twenty leagues from Sâlheyeh; another at El-A'rych, thirty leagues farther on, and one at Gaza, another twenty leagues toward my objective. I had therefore along this line of operation, a distance of 250 leagues, six forts sufficiently strong to secure my communications and resist any enemies that I had to fear. Indeed, in these four campaigns I never had so much as a convoy or a courtier intercepted. . . . The regiments of camels that had been organized in Egypt were so accustomed to the desert that they kept the line of communications open between Cairo and Saint-Jean-d'Acre. With an army of 20,000 men I occupied Egypt, Palestine, and Galilée, some 30,000 leagues shaped like a triangle. From my headquarters before Saint-Jean-d'Acre to General Desaix' headquarters in upper Egypt it was more than 300 leagues.

The campaign of 1800 was conducted along the same principles. When the army of the reserve swung down through the Saint Bernard, I established my first fortified depot at Ivrea; even after Marengo I considered Italy reconquered only when all fortified towns as far as the Mincio were occupied by my troops. . . .

In 1805, having bagged an entire Austrian army 80,000 strong at Ulm, I moved along the Lech, had the old ramparts of Augsburg repaired and armed, built a strong bridgehead over the Lech and made this large city, which afforded me so many resources, my fortified depot. I wanted to rebuild Ulm but the fortifications were razed and the terrain was too unpleasant. From Augsburg I moved along the Inn and seized Braunau. This fortified city secured for me the bridge over this river: it was a second fortified supply depot which permitted me to advance as far as Vienna. This capital itself was fortified against any sudden assault.

I next moved into Moravia and captured the citadel of Brünn, which immediately was armed and provisioned. Located forty leagues from Vienna, it became my base for maneuvering in Moravia. One day's march from this fort I fought the battle of Austerlitz. From this battlefield I could retire to Vienna and cross the Danube there, or else move by the left bank to Linz in order to cross the river over the bridge at this city and reach Braunau.

In 1806 I moved my headquarters to Bamberg and concentrated my entire army on the Regnitz. The Prussian King believed that by moving to the Main River he could sever my line of operation above Mayence and stop my advance . . . but the line of communication of the French army was no longer based upon Mayence. It now went from the fort of Kronach, located at the outlet of the mountains from Saxony, to Forchheim, a fortified city on the Regnitz, and from there to Strasbourg.

Having therefore nothing to fear from the Prussian advance, I debouched in three columns. . . . The Prussian army, between Weimar and Auerstaedt, which already was moving toward the Main to support its advance guard, halted. Cut off from the Elbe and from Berlin, all of its magazines were captured and served to nourish the French army. Before the battle the enemy noticed his danger when his position already was desperate, and although so close to Magdeburg, the heart of his country two marches from the Elbe, he was defeated, split apart, and unable to carry out any retreat. Not one man of this old army of Frederick the Great escaped save for the King and a few squadrons of cavalry. . . .

In 1807, being master of Küstrin, Glogau, and Stettin, I captured Varsovie and through this maneuver cut off Silesia and its fortresses, which, left to their own devices, fell successively. . . . I defeated the Russian army at Eylau, took position on the Passarge to cover the siege of Danzig, which became our main fortified depot and point of support for the operations that preceded the battle of Friedland, which caused the Czar to ask for peace at Tilsit.

In 1808 all of the fortified cities in northern Spain—San Sebastian, Pampeluna, Figueras, Barcelona, and the citadel of Burgos—were at the disposal of the French army when it marched to Madrid, San Sebastian, Pampeluna, Figueras, Barcelona, the citadel at Burgos, and then Girone, Lérida, Mequinenza, Tarragona, Tortosa, Sagonte being at the mercy of Suchet when he marched on Valencie.

In 1809 . . . Augsburg was my center of operations. The Austrians having razed Braunau, I selected the fort at Passau, located on the confluence of the Inn and the Danube and much more advantageous because in one step it assured me the bridge over both rivers. I had it fortified and secured the bridge at Linz with first-class fortifications. Quite apart from this line of communication from Bavaria, my army in Vienna had a secure line of communication from Italy by way of the château at Graetz and the stronghold at Klagenfurt. . . . The works that I ordered to safeguard the passage of the Danube near Wagram have no parallel in history: Caesar's bridge over the Rhine cannot be compared with it.

In 1812, Danzig, Thorn, Modlin, and Prague were my fortified cities on the Vistula; Pillau, Kovno, Bialystoc, and Grodno on the Niemen; Vilna and Minsk on the Dnieper, and Smolensk were my great fortified depots for my movement against Moscow. In this operation I had a fortified base every eight or ten days' march. All post houses were loopholed and intrenched; they were held only by one company and a single gun, which protected the postal service so effectively that throughout the entire campaign not a single courier (there were several each day) or convoy was intercepted. . . . Even in the retreat, except for four days where Admiral Tchitchakof was repulsed beyond the Berezina, the army constantly maintained free communications with its fortified depots.

In 1813 Koenigstein, Dresden, Torgau, Wittenberg, Magdeburg, and Hamburg were my fortified towns on the Elbe, and Merseburg, Erfurt, Würzburg my stages to get to the Rhine.

In the campaign of 1814 I had fortified towns everywhere and they would have been every bit as important as those in Flanders had Paris not fallen as the result of treason.[7]

The Line of Communications in the Russian Campaign

Napoleon's Instructions on the Administrative Services of the Grande Armée, 16 March 1812

The administration of the army is divided into districts—between the Rhine and the Elbe, the Elbe and the Oder, the Oder and the Vistula, and between the Vistula and the Russian frontier.

As for the routes of communication of the army, one will run from Mayence to Magdeburg, thence on to Küstrin and Posen, where it will split into three directions—one to Varsovie, another to Thorn, and the third to Danzig. These routes will be extended as the army advances on the other side of the Vistula.

Another route will go from Wesel to Magdeburg, Berlin, Stettin and Danzig: a branch line will drop down to Dirschau and Marienburg. Another route will go from Hamburg to Stettin. Finally, still another route will go from Mayence to Würzburg, Bamberg, Kronach, Leipzig, Torgau, Glogau, and thence to Posen. From Glogau a branch line will go to Kalisz and to Varsovie.

Another route will go from Innsbruck, Augsburg, and Nuremberg to join the above at Bromberg.

All of these routes are necessary to ease the burden upon the country. An immense movement could not operate along a single route without depleting the surrounding countryside.

There will be no commandants or war commissaries between the Tyrol, the Rhine, and the Elbe. This will be an economy of employees and commandants. . . . [Local princes] will be used in their place. . . . Thus there will be no French gendarmes or employees save for one or two inspectors or war commissioners to make sure that the hospitals and magazines are in good condition and to check on complaints. . . .

There will be hospitals at Brandenburg, Berlin, Küstrin, Stettin, Bromberg, Posen, Glogau, Marienwerder, Marienburg, and Danzig. By following what was done in the last war you will order what is to be established along this line. It is not believed that more than one hospital is needed for every five marches. . . .

The administrative and military headquarters between the Rhine and the Elbe will be at Magdeburg; between the Elbe and the Oder it will be at Berlin; and between the Oder and the Vistula it will be at Posen.[8]

Napoleon to Marshal Berthier, 16 June 1812

The routes of the army between the Vistula and the Niemen will be as follows: at Thorn you will take provisions for two days, which will last as far as Graudenz. The Prussian commandant at Graudenz will supply the provisions for one day to get you to Marienwerder; at Marienwerder the provisions for one day will take you to Marienburg. There the provisions for one day will take you as far as Elbing; at Elbing you will take provisions for three days to last until you reach Koenigsberg. At Koenigsberg you will rest.

You will take provisions for one day as far as Tapiau; at Tapiau, provisions for two days as far as Gumbinnen; at Gumbinnen, two days of provisions as far as Wilkowyszki. Thus the troops will be a dozen days en route from Thorn to Gumbinnen, including the rest at Koenigsberg. They will take a rest at Gumbinnen. This will make thirteen days. None of the intermediate routes will be included. However, you will keep at Osterode a command with a Prussian garrison, a powder magazine, and a bakery, and you will keep 1,000,000 kilograms of flour there. There will be a similar establishment at Rastenburg.

The communication of the army with Varsovie will be thus: you will take at Varsovie two days' provisions to last as far as Pultusk; from there three days will get you to Willenberg, and at Willenberg three days' provisions to take you to Rastenburg, where you will take three days of provisions as far as Gumbinnen. There will be French commanders there, bakeries and flour magazines at Willenberg and Pultusk.

The line of communication with the army from Danzig will be either by Pillau or Marienburg. By Pillau you will take at Danzig provisions for three days as far as Pillau; there you will take provisions for two days as far as Koenigsberg, etc. If the route goes through Marienburg, at Danzig you will take provisions for two days as far as Marienburg, where you will follow the line of communication.

The communication from Koenigsberg to Tilsit will be by taking at Koenigsberg provisions for one day as far as Tapiau; there take on one day's supply as far as Loebau, where you will be provided with two days' provisions as far as Tilsit.

Thus there must be a commandant of the fort at Thorn: he is there. There must be a commandant and a bakery at Marienburg; one exists there and also at Elbing, Koenigsberg, Tapiau, and Insterburg. We need a commandant at Osterode and Willenberg: there is one at Pultusk. We need one at Rastenburg. All other commandants and commissaries of war must be recalled.

We must take care to place French workers in hospitals that must be established and order them to correspond with General Latour at Elbing and with General Hogendorp at Koenigsberg. . . .

You will issue the order for the routes from Marienwerder to Marienburg and Elbing and from Marienburg to Dirschau be repaired and maintained.[9]

Napoleon to Marshal Berthier, 2 July 1812

Assign a general officer of your staff to occupy himself solely with the organization of the routes of communication from Wilkowyszki to Kovno and thence to Vilna. From Wilkowyszki to Kovno you need two commandants and two small garrisons of twenty-five men with one or two gendarmes. They will protect the post, function as police, and regularly forward news of what is happening. They will make the inhabitants repair damaged roads, fill in the quagmires, and repair and maintain the bridges.

From Kovno to Vilna you must assign four commandants and four garrisons each of twenty-five men at Roumchichki, Jijmory, Yevé, and Rykonty. . . . To each post you must add three or four cavalrymen. The commandants will keep us informed on what is happening, have the roads and bridges repaired, and bury the horses and corpses which in this season could cause sickness.

It is also necessary to have, in addition to the staff, two or three battalion commanders or majors who will perform the function of road inspectors: one will be responsible for the road from Wilkowyszki to Kovno and the other from Kovno to Vilna. They will make the rounds of their district twice a week and attend to the maintenance of roads, their police duties, bridge repairs, etc., during the entire time that general headquarters remains at Vilna.

When general headquarters moves forward, the inspector the farthest to the rear will follow in the new direction. Initially the stations must be half a day's distance from each other during the first forty or fifty leagues behind Vilna: you will then reduce them to intervals of one day's distance when the country is organized.[10]

The Campaign of 1805

Napoleon to Prince Eugene, 22 September 1805

It is necessary to aid the army. This is the first duty in our present situation. The army's requisitions in the communes and departments in wheat, wine, fodder, oats, and straw are the only resource that can be used to feed an army of 80,000 men concentrated at a single point. We took this step in Alsace, despite the good organization of the army and the ease with which funds are sent from Paris. All of the prices had reached such a point that it was impossible, even with large sums of money, to meet them. When we had magazines formed a long time in advance, we could sometimes avoid resorting the requisitions, but everywhere else they are indispensable. The Austrians made requisitions in Germany and in Venetia, otherwise one could not feed or supply large armies. Those requisitions made in the communes and departments will be paid for at a reasonable price. . . .

In Alsace I was forced to take measures to requisition vehicles and horses. . . . To impose a penalty against those who hide oats is useless. You must order people to provide oats, and confiscate the oats from those who do not.

Do not worry about these measures displeasing the country. People whine, but they do not mean what they say. They know full well that in circumstances such as these one cannot do otherwise. The Austrians make as many requisitions with these same people and make still more in the Kingdom of Italy. Moreover, they will certainly be convinced that if they do not yield to requisitions the army would take whatever it needed by force and the country would be much worse off. . . .

Be severe, for the good of the army. Hit all of the departments in the Kingdom of Italy with requisitions . . . whether for provisions, fodder, wagons, horses, quarters, or anything else that you might need. Do not be offended by anything. These moments are moments of suffering.[11]

Napoleon to A. M. Petiet, 24 October 1805

We have marched without magazines: circumstances forced us to do it. We have had an extremely favorable season for living off the country but, even though we have been constantly victorious and have found vegetables in the fields, we nonetheless have suffered much.

In a season when there would be no potatoes in the field, or if the army were to experience some reverse, the lack of magazines would cause us the greatest misfortunes.[12]

War must nourish war.[13]

Transport

Napoleon to Pierre-Antoine Daru, Intendant General, 27 March 1808

You will immediately furnish carbines . . . to transport soldiers. . . . I do not see why the teamsters of a convoy, being able to detach their near horse in the team, could not join the escort in defending their wagons. It will be necessary to drill them in the essential infantry maneuvers, such as loading their firearms, firing, and above all marching on foot so that they can guard their convoys. This will contribute significantly both to the safety of the convoys and the honor of the transport corps, for then men will feel a part of the artillery train and the army itself. The officers, even the major inspector, could carry carbines to set the example. I assume that you have given them a general's uniform with a distinctive insignia on the button. . . .

Army corps are composed of two or three divisions. You must attach one transport battalion to each corps of three divisions, one company earmarked for each division and the fourth to be at the disposal of the director of the transport service and the corps staff. . . . Corps comprising two divisions would have three companies . . . with the fourth remaining with the transport battalion. . . .

I intend these caissons to be used solely for transporting bread. For transporting oats, straw, hay, saddles, and disabled men the cavalry has more means than the infantry. . . . No baggage belonging to the officers or generals should be permitted in these wagons. . . .

I assume that the army, if everything is organized as it should be, would have 200 caissons for each corps.[14]

AMMUNITION

Napoleon to Marshal Berthier, 10 April 1809

If the Army of Germany has twice the basic load of artillery stores—whether with the divisions or in the army corps parks, or in the general park—it is in good shape. With twice the usual supply of artillery stores there would be enough on hand to fight three great battles like Austerlitz. To drag along more artillery stores, however, is a useless encumbrance. But there is no question that twice the basic issue of artillery stores would be sufficient, if you had a third in the depot four or five marches to the rear of the army. Thus in the actual situation we should have a reserve of cartridges between Ulm, Donauwoerth, and Ingolstadt in chests that can be carried in the wagons.

If the army marches along the Inn River, for example, this reserve will have to come to Passau, and the army that is on the Inn will have two issues, with a third at Passau. Should the army move to Vienna, it will not find itself more than eight or ten days' distance from its third issue. . . .

It is necessary to have chests that can be carried on the country wagons, five or six days' march behind the army and in places designated to serve as depots. There is no division in the army that does not have transported behind it sixty cartridges for every man carrying a musket. Nor is there an army corps that does not have carried in its park sixty additional rounds for each soldier. Thus, behind each army corps there is a reserve supply of 100 to 120 cartridges for each infantryman.

The general park has more rounds in addition to that. The soldier carries fifty rounds in his sack and has sixty additional rounds in the depots that could arrive within four or five days to replenish the supply that has been consumed. Thus 150 cartridges carried either in the division, the corps, or the general park add up to 15,000,000 cartridges—or ninety caissons—for the army. Fifth rounds in the sack makes 5,000,000 and 5,000,000 in the depots in the rear, in echelons, add up to 25,000,000 cartridges or 200 rounds per man. The depots should be at Ulm, Donauwoerth, Passau, and Ingolstadt, and make the movement in echelons.

To summarize, I am satisfied if the army corps have 10,000 cartridges, either with the division or the army corps park; I am satisfied if the army has 5,000,000 rounds for the soldiers, 5,000,000 rounds with the general park, and another 5,000,000 in reserve to transport by water or in country wagons; finally I am satisfied if there is a single basic load of artillery rounds distributed in the various depots, in echelons, and can be successively replaced.[15]

Convoys

The defense of a convoy will always be difficult, but often the enemy deceives himself as to the strength of a convoy and believes it to be stronger than actually is the case.[16]

It is contrary to every principle . . . to defend the head of the convoy in preference to the rest of it. . . . The tail is the point of greatest need of protection, since the enemy always attacks here. . . . Even if the convoy contains wagons carrying valuable paper, these wagons should be treated no differently from the others, but should be placed under a separate escort.[17]

The cavalry, infantry, and artillery that comprise each convoy should march together, bivouac in a battalion square around the convoy, and never be separated from the convoy under any pretext whatever. . . . No convoy departs if it is not commanded by a field officer and escorted by 1,500 men—infantry and cavalry (not counting the number of transport soldiers, artillery, engineers, or the military transport train).[18] The ordinary convoy escort will be two able-bodied infantrymen, well versed in the *School of the Battalion,* for each wagon in the convoy, one mounted scout for every five wagons and one field piece for every twelve wagons, making in all eighty infantry and eight cavalry for every military transport company, or 240 infantry, twenty-four cavalry and one gun for the military transport battalion. When circumstances require, this escort will be double or even four times as strong, but this will be the regulation size of the convoy. . . .

The company will take only an hour's rest to feed and water the horses; the wagons will be parked on each side of the road . . . in two lines, each wagon fastened one behind the other. . . . The two long sides of this rectangle will be covered by the wagons themselves, the open space in front and rear by . . . the escort. . . . For every five wagons a soldier from the military transport train will be placed in position on one wagon, carbine in hand. . . . The military transport battalion will march in the same manner and take up 2,160 feet of road. . . .

Convoys containing 500 or 600 wagons will park and form two squares, one of three military transport battalions and the other two. . . . These two parks will be formed, insofar as possible, within sight of each other . . . and occupy important positions such as the heads of defiles and bridges . . . so that these . . . are secure. . . . Fieldworks should be erected around these parks every night.[19]

No man is to march alone. They all will be assembled . . . and will depart at times when the convoys are scheduled to leave, to serve as escorts. . . . There must be nearly two convoys per month: that is sufficient.[20]

Evolution of the Marching Battalions

Napoleon to General Berthier, 16 June 1796

Commissary and quartermaster officers are expressly forbidden to issue any marching orders to soldiers who are isolated from their battalions until twenty-five men have been assembled. To this end soldiers who have reported to join their unit will remain assigned for pay and subsistence in the fortified depot until this number has been reached. Then the commissary and quartermaster will issue vouchers and an itinerary to the locale where they will have to separate in order to rejoin their respective units.[21]

Napoleon to General Kellermann, 12 October 1805

As for the men left along the road by the regiments . . . I desire that the troops not be forwarded to me by small detachments, but that a strong detachment of 300 to 400 men be formed from them every eight days which, commanded by an officer . . . will join me in good order.[22]

Napoleon to Marshal Bessières, 16 April 1808

I have already recommended . . . that you establish a basic distinction between *marching* and *provisional* regiments in Spain. A *provisional* regiment of cavalry or infantry is organized and must not undergo any change while it remains in Spain. A *marching* regiment, battalion, or squadron is a temporary organization for the purpose of conducting troops to the provisional regiments at Madrid. . . . Thus you can incorporate all of the isolated men who reach you . . .

into marching regiments or battalions. . . . When you have assembled from 600 to 800 men from one or the other corps, form them into a marching battalion . . . and keep them at Burgos until I send you orders as to their destination. . . .

These precautions are necessary. This army is formed only through constant care and you must not depart from this policy.[23]

Medical Services

If there are tired men in these different columns, send them to a convalescent hospital . . . and leave them there for about a week. In this way you can save men and cut back on illness. You know the importance of that.[24]

In every war, and especially . . . where the strength of the enemy lies in his light cavalry, it is necessary to locate the hospitals in fortified cities.[25] You know how many problems are caused by the evacuation of hospitals. . . . There is nothing worse for the sick than to make them travel, and besides there are men who, separated from their units, are lost.[26] The matter of hospitals is very sensitive. . . . In an army many establishments are prepared, half of which must be useless, but this is in order to keep pace with events.[27]

Order of the Day, 26 September 1796

There will be four [convalescent] depots . . . each assigned to a division. . . . Each of these division commanders will send to its depot a field officer from the division, selected among the auxiliary troops, or recognized for his intelligence and integrity, who will be charged with commanding the depot and corresponding with the division staff. Each demi-brigade will send an officer there. . . . The cavalry has its special depots. The artillery will have a depot at Milan. There would be a gunsmith and a school of arms at each of the four depots. . . . The muskets of all men from the different divisions who go to the hospitals will be sent to the depot.[28]

Napoleon to General Clarke, 24 January 1809

It is a general rule that every man leaving the hospital must return to his unit, if it is on the nearest frontier. He must return to his depot, if his depot is in the military division or on the frontier. He must report at the principal place designated by the minister of war and await orders when the convalescents have to make a long march. . . . Whenever I order you to make a movement you will have to anticipate that for the next two months there will be isolated men to direct. . . . Meanwhile, form a depot.[29]

There should be four kinds of field hospitals—for the regiment, the division, the army corps, and the reserve or main field hospital at general headquarters.

The field hospital of the regiment is composed specifically of a portion of the officers of the medical corps; in matérial, of caissons that the corps must have in return for the advances it has made and the numbers that it handles. This field hospital is under the command of a colonel and must always follow the regiment. This is perhaps of the greatest importance because a good esprit de corps requires that the medical officers be attached to the men and are rewarded by the esteem of the regimental officers. The personnel of this unit consists of two or at most three surgeons and one caisson, and, assuming that each regiment would have four surgeons present, in view of the sick and the unoccupied fortress towns, there would then remain a surgeon for the division ambulance, which would be nearly four surgeons for the division hospital.

The second kind of field hospital is the division field hospital, which should have administrators . . . medical officers, and equipment consisting of two caissons. The obvious flaw in this organization is that it is necessary that the commander of this field hospital belong to no regiment, so that he is impartial and will not deprive a unit of its surgeon major. It should therefore be necessary . . . to have a surgeon major *extraordinaire* for each division.

The field hospitals for the army corps are called light hospitals, because they are mounted.[30]

EYLAU CAMPAIGN, 1806

Everything points to the belief . . . that we will have a large battle here within the next three or four days. It is therefore essential to take every measure relative to field hospitals: where are they, what is their condition, and where are the surgeons? It is a very important matter which has never been sufficiently anticipated in our battles, and that is to have, apart from the field hospitals, some brigades of country wagons, with straw, entrusted to several agents, for going over the battlefield and gathering up the wounded immediately after the action.

It would be useful to have ten of these brigades of ten wagons each, which would be 100 wagons. These must be independent of the field hospitals and whatever is attached to them. It is the surest and the most necessary means, but for it to be really useful these wagons must be on the battlefield as soon as the fighting has ended, so that all of the wounded are evacuated before night.

I repeat, however, that it is essential that this be independent of the ordinary ambulances and of all other means of evacuating the wounded.[31]

MARCH DISCIPLINE

Order of the Day, 14 May 1809

The Emperor is painfully aware of the disorders committed in the rear of the army: they have reached the point that they have forced themselves on his attention. Poor subjects seek to dishonor the army, and instead of moving to their colors and facing the enemy, they remain in the rear where they commit every excess and even crimes.

His Majesty orders the governor generals commanding the provinces to form mobile columns immediately, each composed of an adjutant commander or colonel, a cavalry major, an infantry captain, and an officer of military police [*gendarme*] . . . and a local magistrate.

These officers will form as many military commissions as there are mobile columns. . . . Behind these commissions . . . there will be three brigades of gendarmes, each consisting of sixty mounted men and ninety infantry.

Every straggler who, under the guise of fatigue, detaches himself from his unit to maraud will be arrested, judged by a military commission, and executed within the hour. . . .

These columns with a strength no greater than 150 men will be divided into small patrols . . . in order to go wherever necessary.[32]

Army Order, 22 June 1812

Each marshal or corps commander will name a provost commission composed of five officers, which will try every soldier who, following the army, is absent from his regiment without a legitimate reason and every marauder and individual caught pillaging or molesting the local inhabitants. This commission will condemn the guilty to death and will have them executed in twenty-four hours.

A provost's commission consisting of five officers, around which a mobile column will be formed consisting of 200 local inhabitants, ten gendarmes, and forty French cavalry, will be established at Maryampol for the Department of Lomza.[33]

The mobile column will be commanded by a French general or field officer and will be subdivided into ten small columns or patrols, each twenty-five men strong, which will cover the country in every direction and arrest every straggler or marauder, and everyone who instigates disorders. Those arrested will be led before the Provost's Commission at Maryampol and, if judge guilty, will be condemned. . . .

Commanders of the different posts and crossings over the Oder and Vistula . . . are expressly forbidden to allow any individual soldier to cross. Individual men leaving the hospitals, convalescents, or absent from their units under any pretext whatever, will be held by the commandants of Glogau, Küstrin, and Stettin until they have been able to assemble 100 armed and well-clothed men to form a company, which they will direct to the forts on the Vistula.[34]

When the army has crossed the Niemen . . . you will designate two or three points where all men returning from the hospitals must be assembled, and from which they will not leave until they are well armed and well clothed.[35]

Occupation of Conquered Territory

The conduct of a general in conquered territory is surrounded with dangers. If he is harsh he aggravates and increases the numbers of his enemies. If he is soft, he inspires hope that later intensifies the abuses and annoyances inevitably attached to the state of war. In either case, if a riot in these circumstances is quelled in time, and if the conqueror knows how to blend severity, justice, and mildness, it would only have a good effect.

Disarm the country: do it thoroughly. Occupy the fortresses: turn the mortar batteries upon the towns. Arm and provision the fortresses so that anyone may be able to defend them.[36] In your calculations assume that fifteen days sooner or later you will have an insurrection. That is something that constantly occurs in conquered territory.[37]

I would certainly desire that the *canaille* . . . revolt. As long as you have not made an example of anyone you will never be master. An entire conquered people find it necessary to revolt, and I should regard a revolt . . . in the the same way as the father of a family looks upon smallpox in his children: provided it does not excessively weaken the inflicted, it is a beneficial crisis.[38]

All persons who have committed excesses, and stirred up rebellion, either by setting up any rallying signal for the crowd, or by exciting it against the French, or the government, must be brought before a military tribunal and instantly shot. Two or three examples are indispensable, and must be made.[39] Every spy . . . [and] every leader of a riot must be shot.[40]

As a general rule, it is a political principle to create a good impression of your benevolence after having demonstrated that you can be severe with troublemakers.[41] Get rid of the prominent men; punish the smallest fault with severity.[42] All foreign people, but especially the Italians, need severe repression from time to time.[43] There is no doubt that you have nothing to fear from the moneyed classes, but . . . [44] the ignorance of the mountain people is such that they interpret the absence of punishment as weakness and . . . the consequences of this are always very dangerous.[45] Make the grandees and other influential people of the country understand thoroughly that the fate of . . . the country . . . depends on their behavior.[46] Hostages are one of the most effective ways to . . . keep conquered provinces under control . . . when the people are persuaded that the death of these hostages would be the immediate result of a breach of their loyalty.[47]

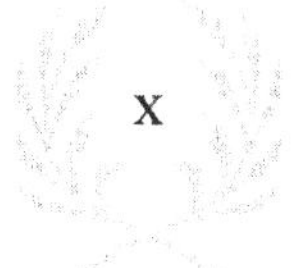

X

The Operational Art

Traditionally soldiers have divided military activity into strategy and tactics. But in 1982 the U.S. Army doctrinal training manual defined war as a national undertaking to be coordinated at three *basic levels of execution—strategic,* operational, *and tactical. The operational level now became the theory of larger unit operations involving planning and conducting campaigns. Napoleon would have had little difficulty with this definition. He would have agreed with General Burnod of the Russian army, one of his translators, who observed: "The art of war is susceptible of being considered under two titles: the one, which rests entirely on the knowledge and genius of the commander; the other, on matters of detail. The first is the same for . . . the Great Captains of all centuries. The matters of detail, on the contrary, are subject to the influence of time, to the spirit of the people and the character of armaments."*

Selected Maxims Relating to the Operational Art

(3) An army invading a country may either have its two wings resting on neutral countries or on great natural obstacles, such as rivers or chains of mountains; or it may have only one of its wings thus supported; or both may be without support.

In the first case, a general has only to see that his line is not broken in front. In the second case, he must rest on the wing which is supported. In the third case, he must keep his different corps resting well on his center and never allow them to separate from it; for if it is a disadvantage to have two flanks in the air, the inconvenience is doubled if there are four, tripled if there are six; that is to say, if an army is divided into two or three distinct corps.

The line of operation in the first case may rest on the left or the right wing, indifferently. In the second case, it should rest on the wing which is supported. In the third case, it should fall perpendicularly on the middle of the line formed by the army in marching. But in all three cases . . . it is necessary to have at every five or six days' march, a fort or intrenched position, where magazines of provisions and military stores may be established and convoys organized, and which may serve as a center of motion and a point of supply, and thus shorten the line of operation.

(4) It may be laid down as a principle that in invading a country with two or three armies, each of which has its own distinct line of operation extending toward a fixed point at which all are to unite, the union of the different corps should never be ordered to take place in the vicinity of the enemy, as by concentrating his forces he may not only prevent their junction but also defeat them one by one.

(6) At the commencement of a campaign, the question whether to advance or not requires careful deliberation, but once you have undertaken the offensive, it should be maintained to the last extremity. A retreat, however skillful the maneuvers may be, will always produce an injurious moral effect on the army, since by losing the chances of success yourself you throw them into the hands of the enemy. Besides, retreats cost far more in men and matériel than the most bloody engagements, except that in a battle the enemy loses nearly as much as you, while in a retreat the loss is all on your side.

(7) An army should be every day, every night, and every hour, ready to offer all the resistance of which it is capable. It is necessary, therefore, that the soldiers should always have

their arms and ammunition at hand, that the infantry should always have with it its artillery, cavalry, and generals, that the different divisions of the army should be always in a position to assist, support, and protect each other; that whether encamped, marching, or halted, the troops should be always in advantageous positions, possessing the qualities required for every field of battle—that is to say, the flanks should be well supported and the artillery so placed that it may all be brought into play.

When the army is in column of march, there must be advance guards and flank guards to observe the enemy's movements . . . and at sufficient distances to allow the main body of the arm to deploy and take up its position.

(8) A general should say to himself many times a day: "If the hostile army were to make its appearance in front, on my right, or on my left, what should I do?" And if he is embarrassed, his arrangements are bad; there is something wrong; he must rectify his mistake.

(10) When your army is inferior in numbers, inferior in cavalry and in artillery, a pitched battle should be avoided. The want of numbers must be supplied by rapidness in marching; the want of artillery by the character of the maneuvers; the inferiority in cavalry by the choice of positions. . . .

(11) To operate upon lines remote from each other and without communications between them is a fault which ordinarily occasions a second. The detached column has orders only for the first day. Its operations for the second day depend on what has happened to the main body. Thus, according to circumstances, the column wastes its time waiting for orders or it acts at random.

It ought then to be adopted as a principle that the columns of an army should be always kept united, so that the enemy cannot thrust himself between them. When for any reason this maxim is departed from, the detached corps should be independent in their operations. They should move toward a fixed point at which they are to unite . . . [and] march without hesitation and without new orders, and should be exposed as little as possible to the danger of being attacked separately.

(12) An army should have but a single line of operation, which it should carefully preserve, and should abandon only when compelled by imperious circumstances.

(14) Among mountains there are everywhere numerous positions extremely strong by nature, which you should abstain from attacking. The genius of this kind of war consists in occupying camps either on the flank or the rear of the enemy, so as to leave him no alternative but to withdraw from his position without fighting; and to move him farther back, or to make him come out and attack you.

In mountain war the attacking party acts under a disadvantage. Even in offensive war, the merit lies in having only defensive conflicts and obliging your enemy to become the assailant.

(16) A well-established maxim of war is not to do anything which your enemy wishes—and for the single reason that he does so wish.

You should therefore avoid a field of battle which he has reconnoitered and studied. You should be still more careful to avoid one which he has fortified and where he has intrenched himself. A corollary of this principle is, never to attack in front a position which admits of being turned.

(17) In a war of marches and maneuvers, to escape an engagement with a superior enemy it is necessary to throw up intrenchments every night and to place yourself always in a good position for defense. The natural positions which are commonly met with cannot secure an army against the superiority of a more numerous one without the aid of art.

(18) An ordinary general occupying a bad position, if surprised by a superior force, seeks safety in retreat; but a Great Captain displays the utmost determination and advances to meet the enemy. By this movement he disconcerts his adversary; and if the march of the latter evinces irresolution, an able general, profiting by the moment of indecision, may yet hope for victory, or at least employ the day in maneuvering, and at night he can intrench himself or fall back on a better position. . . .

(19) The passage from the defensive to the offensive is one of the most delicate operations of war.

(20) Your line of operation should never, as a general rule, be abandoned, but changing it when circumstances require is one of the most skillful of military maneuvers. An army that changes its line of operation skillfully deceives the enemy, who no longer knows where his antagonist's rear is, or what are the weak points to threaten.

(21) When an army is encumbered with siege equipage and large convoys of wounded and sick, it should approach its depots by the shortest roads and as expeditiously as possible.

(22) The art of encamping on a position is nothing else than the art of forming in order of battle on that position. For this purpose the artillery should all be in readiness and favorably placed; a position should be selected which is not commanded, cannot be turned, and from which the ground in the vicinity is covered and commanded.

(23) When you occupy a position which the enemy threatens to surround, you should collect your forces quickly and menace him with an offensive movement. By this maneuver you prevent him from detaching a part of his troops and annoying your flanks, in case you should deem a retreat indispensable.

(24) A military maxim, which ought never to be neglected, is to assemble your cantonments at the point that is most remote and best sheltered from the enemy, especially when he makes his appearance unexpectedly. You will then have time to unite the whole army before he can attack you.

(26) It is a violation of correct principles to cause corps to act separately, without communication with each other, in the face of a concentrated army with easy communications.

(27) When you are driven from your first position, the rallying point of your columns should be so far in the rear that the enemy cannot get there before them. It would be the greatest of disasters to have your columns attacked one by one before their reunion.

(28) No detachment should be made the day preceding a battle, for during the night the state of things may change, either by a retreat of the enemy or by the arrival of strong reinforcements. . . .

(29) When you have it in contemplation to give battle, it is a gen-

eral rule to collect all your strength and to leave none unemployed. One battalion sometimes decides the issue of the day.

(36) When a hostile army is covered by a river on which it has several bridgeheads, you should not approach it in front, for in doing so your forces would be too little concentrated and in danger of being broken into detached parts, if the enemy should sally from one of the bridgeheads.

You should approach the river you wish to cross in columns disposed in echelon, so that there may be only a single column—the foremost one—which the enemy can attack without exposing his own flank. Meanwhile the light troops will line the bank; and when you have fixed on the point at which to pass, you must proceed rapidly to the spot and throw the bridge across. You must take care that the bridge shall always be at a distance from the leading echelon in order to deceive the enemy.

(40) Fortresses are useful in offensive as well as defensive war. Undoubtedly they cannot of themselves arrest the progress of an army, but they are an excellent means of delaying, impeding, enfeebling, and annoying a victorious enemy.

(64) Nothing is more important in war than unity in command. When, therefore, you are carrying on hostilities against a single power only, you should have but one army acting on one line and led by one commander.

(82) With a great general there is never a continuity of great actions which can be attributed to chance and good luck; they always are the result of calculation and genius.

(95) In war there is but one favorable moment; the great art is to seize it.[1]

At the moment war is declared there is so much to do that it is wise to begin preparation several years in advance.[2] I am in the habit of thinking three or four months in advance about what I must do, and to master the secrets of the art of war. I calculate on the basis of the worst possible case.[3] If I take so many precautions it is because my custom is to leave nothing to chance.[4]

In war it is necessary to have sound and precise ideas.[5] It is with safe and well-conceived plans that we win wars.[6] There is no man more pusillanimous than I when it comes to planning a campaign. I purposely exaggerate all the dangers and all the calamities that the circumstances make possible. I am in a thoroughly painful state of agitation. This does not keep me from looking quite serene in front of my entourage; I am like an unmarried girl laboring with child. Once I have made up my mind, everything is forgotten except what leads to success.[7]

The art of war is a simple art and everything depends upon execution: there is nothing vague, everything is common sense, and nothing about it is ideological.[8] The art of war consists, with an inferior army, of always having more forces than your enemy at the point where you attack, or at the point which is attacked; but this art cannot be learned either from books or from practice. It is a feeling of command which properly constitutes the genius for war.[9]

Every offensive war is a war of invasion, and every war conducted according to the rules of the art is a methodical war.[10]

In an art as difficult as the art of war, the scheme of a battle is often implicit in the scheme of the campaign. Only the most experienced soldiers would understand that. . . . In the Moravian campaign [1806] I understood that the Russians, having no general of the first rank, would believe that the French army would retreat upon Vienna. They had to make it a high priority to intercept this road, when in fact the retreat of the army throughout the Moravian campaign had never been intended to be toward Vienna. This single circumstance distorted all of the enemy's calculations and inevitably contributed to those movements that led to his defeat.[11]

Do not be surprised at the attention that I devote to details: I must pay attention to everything so as never to leave myself unprovided.[12]

Marshal Berthier to General Gouvion Saint-Cyr, by order of the Emperor, 2 September 1805

I do not believe that I am bound to wait until the last moment to let you know the plan of campaign adopted by the Emperor. It is well that you are instructed fifteen days in advance so that, in the greatest silence, you can take all your measures, and when I will have transmitted the Emperor's final orders to commence hostilities you will be prepared to play the important role that His Majesty has entrusted in you in his vast plans, which extend from the Baltic as far as Naples.

You will have 20,000 men at the moment hostilities begin—French, Poles, Swiss, or Italians. This force, sufficient to seize Naples, expel the court, and break up and destroy the Neapolitan army, will not be larger if 12,000 Russians and 6,000 English have the time to act in concert with the Neapolitan army from Corfu and Malta.

It is essential that you have the initiative in movements: you therefore must gain time, dissimulate your projects soundly, and that up to the moment when your operations commence, give the King of Naples no cause for any uneasiness. . . .

Your operations can be considered from two points of view: with respect to the Neapolitan army, you are attacking and you must wage offensive war, invade the kingdom, and if superior coalition forces should desire . . . to wage offensive war in the Kingdom of Naples, you will function as a corps of observation that will contest the terrain but not conquer, for they will be far superior to you. You will make their conquest difficult and their march slow, and thus gain time for the armies of Germany and Italy to send you numerous and strong reinforcements. . . . Your operations therefore are of little utility for the strategic operations, but from the point of view of an army of observation opposed to a coalition, you will prevent, or considerably retard, their junction with the Austrian Army of the Adige.

The great blows will be struck in Germany, where the Emperor will move in person, and the operations even of the Army of Italy, if they do not succeed, must have no influence upon your own operations. . . . If the Emperor's operations are crowned with the success that we have a right to expect, their first result will be to rescue the Army of Italy and to send you the help that you will need to throw the forces of the coalition into the sea, retake all the country that you will have lost, and even threaten Sicily.

In the final analysis, you must begin the armament and provisioning of Pescara at once, place all of your depots of your army there, and appoint a *commandant d'armes.*

It is on this point that you will direct your relief and finally it is your center of gravity. This fortress must be held for several months, even if you are forced to evacuate the entire country, and give the Emperor the time needed to complete his plan.[13]

Notes for the King of Spain [Joseph], September 1808

First Observation. It is proposed to march on Madrid with 50,000 men by being united and abandoning the communications with France.

The military art is an art that has principles that must never be violated. To change one's line of operation is an operation of genius: to lose it is an operation so serious that it renders the general guilty of it a criminal. Thus, to guard one's line of operation it is necessary to reach a fortress where there is a depot and one can find provisions, rally the troops, and get rid of his prisoners and the sick and wounded.

If, being at Madrid, we could have concentrated our forces in the city, we could have regarded the Retiro as a concentrated place for hospitals, prisoners, and as a means for holding a large city and saving the resources that it offers; that would have been to lose our communications with France but to assure our line of operation; especially if we could have taken advantage of the time to collect a great quantity of provisions and munitions, and had fortresses made to serve as *points d'appui* and outposts for divisions every one or two marches at the principal debouches, like the citadel of Sagovie. But today, since we are cooped up in the interior of Spain without having any organized center, no magazine formed, with enemy armies on the flanks and in the rear, it would be a great folly without precedent in the history of the world.

If, before taking Madrid and organizing the army there, with magazines for eight to ten days and sufficient munitions, we had been defeated, what would have happened to this army? Where could it have rallied? Where would it evacuate its wounded? Where could it draw its munitions of war or even a simple victualing? Need more be said? Those who dare recommend such a measure would be the first to lose their head as soon as events would have exposed the folly of their operation.

When one is in a besieged fortress, he has lost his line of communication, but not his line of operation, because the line of operation is from the glacis to the center of the fortress, where the hospitals, magazines, and means of subsistence are located. If one is defeated from without? Then he rallies at the glacis, and he has three or four hours to prepare the troops and reorganize their morale. . . .

I can only repeat what has been stated time and again. Attack the enemy if he approaches within two marches. Should you obtain a decisive victory against all of his united forces or several victories against his isolated units, these must determine the course that you will take. But all these combats must be fought according to the rules of war, that is to say, with your line of communication secure.[14]

Napoleon to Eugene Napoleon, Viceroy of Italy, at Gönyö. Schoenbrunn, 19 June 1809

The plan that you presented me for crossing the left bank of the Danube vis-à-vis the position where you are now is impractical. I would not go into any details if I were not persuaded that you read my letters with attention and that you would benefit from the contents for your instruction.

It is six marches from your present position to Vienna. Even if I had a bridge at your location I would not cross the Danube there, because while making the passage Prince Charles [of Lorraine], with the main Austrian army, would cross the river behind me, at Vienna. In two days he would have made a bridge. But Raab is not as good as Vienna. My center and my line of communication would be severed and I would find myself in an unfortunate position.

If I wished to cross the Danube at such a great distance from Vienna, what would prevent me from crossing at Linz, where I have a superb bridge and would find myself in a much better position, because I would cover my rear and would have nothing to fear in front of me, seeing that the Traun and Enns rivers would cover Linz? For this reason I would not cross in the position that you indicated, even if I had a stone bridge.

Actually, why dream of crossing in front of Raab, having nothing on our side that could cover Buda and all of Hungary, and would guarantee my line of communication from your location with Vienna? For you have no position on this side. Even assuming that I crossed the left bank, where would I march then? Against the whole Austrian army? I would not find it there: it would be on the right bank, making itself master of Vienna and, together with Hungarians from Buda, proceeding to attack my bridgehead on the right bank. And besides, it would require another corps to keep under observation from the direction of Komorn, which would be a great and terrible inconvenience.

The plan that you present is therefore based upon false reasoning, for it is nothing to cross the Danube. I have a bridge at Passau, and one at Linz. If I wished to throw a bridge on the left bank from your side it would have to be done above Raab, in order to be protected by this village which we assume to be occupied by ourselves.[15]

The Influence of Terrain

The frontiers that defend empires consist of plains, hilly country, and mountains. Should an army desire to cross them and is superior in cavalry, it will do well to take its line of operation across the plains. If inferior in the mounted arm, it will prefer hilly country; but for the mountainous terrain it will be satisfied in every case by keeping the mountains in view while turning them.

In fact, a line of operation must not cross through mountainous terrain because

1. An army cannot supply itself there
2. In mountainous country an army encounters at every step defiles that it would have to occupy by fortresses
3. The march there is difficult and slow
4. Columns of brave men can be held up there by ragged peasants, leaving the clodhopper to be conquered and vanquished
5. The knack of mountain warfare is never to attack, for even when one wishes to conquer he must open the road by maneuvers of position that leave the army corps charged with the

defense no alternative than to attack or to fall back; and finally

6. Because a line of operation must serve as a line of retreat, and how does one propose to retreat through gorges, defiles, and precipices?

It happens that large armies, when they cannot do otherwise, have crossed mountainous country to reach fine plains and favorable country. Thus it becomes necessary to cross the Alps to reach Italy. But to make supernatural efforts to cross unapproachable mountains and then find oneself still in the middle of precipices, defiles, and boulders, with no other prospect than to have similar obstacles to overcome for a long while, to endure the same fatigues and to be uneasy in each new march for knowing that there are so many bad steps behind you . . . is to act contrary to common sense and therefore is contrary to the spirit of the art of war. Your enemy has large cities, beautiful provinces, and capitals to protect. March there by way of the plains.

Of all the obstacles that can cover the frontiers of empires, a desert like the Syrian desert is unquestionably the greatest. Mountain ranges such as the Alps hold the second rank, and rivers the third, because if one has so much trouble transporting provisions for an army, which one rarely succeeds in doing completely, this difficulty increases twentyfold when an army must drag along water, forage, and wood—three items that weigh a great deal, are very difficult to transport, and which armies ordinarily find on the spot.

Throughout history we see that those generals marching from Egypt to Syria, or from Syria to Egypt, have considered this desert as an obstacle that grows in proportion to the number of horses with the army. According to the ancient historians, when Cambyses wished to invade Egypt he made an alliance with an Arab king, who cut a canal of water in the desert, which evidently is a way of saying that he covered the desert with a stream of camels carrying water. Alexander the Great tried to please the Jews so that they might be of service to him in crossing the desert. However, this obstacle in ancient times was not as formidable as it is today, since towns and villages existed then and the industry of man had struggled against these difficulties with effect. Today there remains nearly nothing from Sâlheyeh as far as Gaza. An army must therefore cross it in stages by forming settlements and magazines at Sâlheyeh, Qatyeh, and El-A'rych. Should this army leave Syria, it must first form a large magazine at El-A'rych, and then move it to Qatyeh. But these operations, being very slow, give the enemy time to make his defensive preparations.[16]

It is a very exhausting and extremely delicate operation to cross the desert in the summer. The heat of the sand, the lack of water and of shade can cause an army to perish or to be weakened and discouraged beyond what can possibly be imagined. In the winter this obstacle is much less formidable. You no longer have the inconvenience of the heat of the sand nor the intolerable heat of the sun, and you require less water.

It is therefore easy to understand that a fortified village at El-A'rych, which would prevent the enemy from using the wells and camping under the shade of the palms, would be very valuable. The army that wanted to besiege it would have to camp exposed to the heat of the sun and receive its provisions, forage, wood, fascines, and water from Gaza. And once El-A'rych is taken it would then require many weeks to provision this magazine to the point where it could supply all of the needs of the army during the siege of Qatyeh. . . .

Before daring to leave Qatyeh, one would have to form great magazines there that could supply the needs of the army in its march as far as Sâlheyeh. This army, weakened by crossing the desert from Qatyeh to Sâlheyeh, could be defeated by a smaller force. If defeated before reaching Cairo, it has only a single line of retreat, and it is encumbered by a large number of camels carrying water. An army defeated and thrown back into the desert can no longer take position.[17] War is a profession of positions.[18]

In mountain warfare it is necessary to await the attack and not take the offensive. That is the trick. If the enemy occupies a strong position you must occupy a position that will force him to attack you. . . . Mountains are greater obstacles than rivers. One can always cross a river, but not a mountain. Often, as in the Vosges, there are only two or three places to cross and yet these are barred by fortresses that prevent anyone from crossing. A bridge can be thrown up in several hours; it takes six months to establish a road. At Marengo I would have had to cross the Alps had the King of Sardinia not traced the routes as far as the foothills. Had there been enough men to defend the village and the fort of Bard, I could not have crossed.

In the mountains one finds everywhere a large number of extremely strong positions in themselves. . . . The genius of this kind of war consists in occupying the camps or the flanks or the rear of the enemy, which gives him the alternative of evacuating his positions without fighting to occupy others farther to the rear, or to evacuate or leave them to attack you. In mountain warfare, he who attacks is at a disadvantage. Even in offensive warfare, the art consists in fighting only defensively and forcing the enemy to attack.[19]

APPENDIX

Critical Analysis: The Wars of Frederick the Great

"Theory will have fulfilled its main task when it is used to analyze the constituent elements of war, to distinguish precisely what at first sight seems fused, to explain in full the properties of the means employed and to show their probable effects, to define clearly the nature of the ends in view, and to illuminate all phases of warfare in a thorough critical inquiry." So wrote Carl von Clausewitz, one of the foremost military theorists to emerge from the Napoleonic wars. His insights came mostly from a careful analysis of the campaigns of Frederick the Great and Napoleon. Instead of looking to military history for a specific doctrine, which was typical of many theorists of his day, Clausewitz looked to theory to provide the framework for a serious study of war. "Theory," he asserted, "should not be expected to provide specific rules to accompany an officer in the field; rather its function is primarily to guide the future commander in his self-education." In applying his theory to historical studies Clausewitz used a method that he called Critical Analysis—"the application of theoretical truths to actual events."

Only when a soldier comprehends the motives, apprehensions, and problems confronting a commander in the past is he fully able to cultivate his own talents. "The man who means to move in such a medium as the element of war," wrote Clausewitz, "should bring with him nothing from books but the general education of his understanding. *If he extracts . . . cut-and-dried ideas that are not derived from the impulse of the moment, the stream of events will dash his structure to the ground before it is finished. He will never be intelligible to . . . men of natural genius; and least of all will he inspire confidence in the most distinguished among them, those who know their own wishes and intentions." But experience alone, even with its wealth of "lessons," could "never produce a Newton or an Euler."*

Napoleon would have agreed with Clausewitz—indeed, he may well have been Clausewitz' inspiration—for as he commented to one of the generals accompanying him into exile to Saint Helena, "My son should read and meditate often about history . . . the only true philosophy. And he should read and think about the wars of the Great Captains. This is the only way to learn about war."

THE CAMPAIGN OF 1756

I. Austria, France, and Russia were ill disposed toward Prussia. Austria regretted the loss of Silesia, France felt resentment over the peace of Dresden, which had caused the disasters of Marshal Belle-Isle, abandoned in Prague; and the Czarina, who was won over by Maria Theresa, was attempting to intervene in the affairs of Europe. It was time, people asserted in Vienna, Paris, and St. Petersburg, to put a check on the ambition of the second-rate powers.

Seeing this approaching storm, Frederick leaned on England, concluding a treaty of alliance between the two powers and assuring himself of rich subsidies. That done, he lost no time and in the summer of 1756, observing that his enemies were still dissembled because they were not yet ready to take the field, he began hostilities without a declaration of war and invaded Saxony in a time of peace.

His military establishment was considerably augmented. He had had ten years to capitalize on the experience acquired in the four campaigns in the War of the Pragmatic Sanction, and the resources that the rich provinces of Silesia had provided him. He had no less than 120,000 men under arms, well organized, well disciplined, and very mobile, apart from his garrisons, depots, and all the additional means to maintain such a considerable army in active service and to make good his losses. Austria had a military establishment of less than 40,000 men, poorly organized and equipped, its veteran troops having been destroyed in the war against the Turks. Frederick could undertake anything in this campaign with impunity.

He united two armies, one in Saxony comprising seventy battalions of infantry and eighty squadrons of cavalry, 64,000 men in all, including artillery and sappers; and the other in Silesia, with thirty-three battalions and fifty-five squadrons, about 30,000 men; and he employed 20,000 men in diverse corps of observation on the Vistula, in Pomerania, and on the lower Elbe. The Army of Silesia assembled at Náchod under the command of Marshal Schwerin and the three corps of the Army of Saxony were assembled at Frankfurt on the Oder, Magdeburg, and Wittenberg. They commenced their march on 30 August, the corps at Magdeburg by Leipzig, Chemnitz, and Dippoldiswalde; that from Wittenberg by Torgau and Meissen, and the corps from Frankfurt by Elsterwerda, Bautzen, and Stolpen.

The alarm was great in Dresden. The Elector took refuge in the fortress of Koenigstein while the Electress and the court remained at the palace. The Saxon army, 18,000 strong, encamped at Pirna to await the decisions of the Court of Vienna. The acquisition of Dresden was an important conquest for the Prussian King, for he found there all the war magazines and the arsenal of the Elector. The fortress was strong; it provided the fulcrum that he needed, and it completed the frontier of the Elbe, which now was under his control the entire way from Magdeburg.

All negotiations to win over the Elector and induce the submission of his army having failed, Frederick advanced and surrounded the camp at Pirna with forty-two battalions and ten squadrons. He formed an army of observation of twenty-eight battalions and seventy squadrons, assumed command, and moved his headquarters to Aussig, in Bohemia. Marshal Schwerin advanced to within a day's march of the Army of Silesia to observe the debouche of Koeniggraetz.

II. Upon the first report that the Prussian army was assembling, the Court of Vienna had united all of its troops and formed them into two corps: one, under the command of Prince Piccolomini, encamped near Koeniggraetz to oppose the movements of Schwerin, while the other, under the orders of Marshal Browne, initially united at Kolin, then later crossed the Moldau and encamped at Budin on the Eger, to rescue the Saxons at the camp of Pirna.

On 30 September Frederick left his camp at Aussig and marched to meet Browne. That evening he reached the village of Lobositz with his advance guard, eight battalions and fifteen squadrons, where he encountered the Austrian army that had just crossed the Eger and encamped behind the marsh within sight of Lobositz. He took position with his advance guard at the village of Turmitz, and was joined there by the rest of his army, 25,000 strong, during the night.

At daybreak Browne ordered a strong body of cavalry to debouch into the plain. Frederick's army took up arms: the left, under the command of the Duke of Bevern, occupied the heights of Lobosch; and the right, under Prince Henry, the heights of Homolka. His line of battle was from 3,200 to 4,000 yards in length. Marshal Browne's front was covered by a marshy stream; his right rested on the Elbe, his left at Tschirschkowiz. His line of battle was 5,000 yards. Recognizing the mistake he had committed in not occupying the heights of Lobosch, he launched an attack with a division of eleven battalions, which was repulsed. The Prussians captured Lobositz, and the Austrians resumed the position they had occupied that morning. They were unassailable in front, but as a result of maneuvers against their left they evacuated, recrossing the Eger and returned to their camp at Budin, having lost 2,500 to 3,000 men. The Prussians lost from 3,000 to 3,500.

Both armies claimed the victory, Marshal Browne because he had not been driven from his camp, and Frederick, more deservedly, because he had captured the village of Lobositz and forced the enemy to give up his plan to relieve the Saxons by the left bank of the Elbe. However, on 11 October Browne detached 8,000 men opposite Koenigstein by the right bank, in sight of the Prussian army, to assist in raising the blockade of the camp of Pirna. The Saxons crossed the Elbe but, enveloped on all sides by the Prussians, they capitulated on the 14th. The Elector executed his option to retire into his Kingdom of Poland and the Saxons were incorporated into the Prussian army, which evacuated Bohemia and took up winter quarters in Saxony and Silesia. . . .

III. First Observation. Some military writers have asserted that Frederick should have penetrated through Moravia to Vienna and ended the war by capturing this capital. They are in error. He could have been stopped by the fortresses of Olmütz and Brunn, and upon reaching the Danube he could have found all of the forces of the monarchy reunited to dispute his passage, while the Hungarian insurrection would have attacked his flanks.

Such a rash operation would have exposed his army to certain ruin. To invade Saxony, capture Dresden, disarm the Saxon army, enter Bohemia, occupy Prague, and go into winter quarters there was all that he could do—or should have done. But he performed poorly, disregarding several of the principles of war that one rarely violates with impunity. This was the reason why he failed in spite of winning the battle.

The camp at Pirna was 50,000 yards in circumference. The 18,000 Saxons were reduced to 14,000 men of all arms upon reaching the camp. Frederick, with forces four times this strength and provided with as much heavy artillery that one could desire, since the arsenal at Dresden was at his disposal, ought to have forced this camp in four days and compelled the Saxons to lay down their arms, and then entered Bohemia, leaving only a garrison of six battalions and six squadrons in Dresden. The camp at Pirna is defended on the east by the Elbe, an unfordable river 120 to 180 yards wide; on the west by a precipitous marsh of considerable depth and sixty to ninety-six yards wide; and finally, at the head, by the fortress of Koenigstein and some woods and ravines that extended to the Bohemian frontier. It formed a large triangle, with two sides stretching from 20,000 to 22,000 yards, and the short side from 6,000 to 8,000 yards.

The 14,000 Saxons were too weak to defend such an extensive line. Had Frederick made nine attacks, three on each side, only one of them being the real assault in one of the places where the ravine juts out, by placing two batteries of fifty guns each, he would have succeeded in taking the ravine. It would have required only fifteen minutes to build a slope there through which two thirds of his army—infantry, cavalry, and artillery—could debouch. Once the Saxons were driven under the walls of Koenigstein they would have surrendered. To be sure, an army of 40,000 men, fighting an army of 60,000 to 80,000, can defend itself successfully in the camp at Pirna, but 14,000 men could not defend themselves against an army of 60,000 that was provided with as much artillery as it wanted. Such a weak body of troops could have defended itself only if the ravine and the Elbe, which covered the camp, had been 400 to 600 yards wide, which would have allowed the batteries of the camp to take positions 400 yards from the bank with nothing to fear from the superior Prussian batteries in position on the opposite bank and yet all-powerful against any force that might be approaching their own side of the river

Second Observation. Frederick entered Bohemia with two *corps d'armée* separated from each other by a considerable distance. Schwerin's army operated at the extremity of Silesia while Frederick was moving into Bohemia along the left bank of the Elbe. This method of invading a country with a double line of operation is faulty. Schwerin was much stronger than Piccolomini both in number and in the composition of his troops. Had he been with Frederick on the battlefield of Lobositz, the reinforcement that Piccolomini had brought to Marshal Browne would have far from compensated for the amount of strength that the Prussian army would have gained. Frederick might therefore have entered Prague in September with 90,000 men, made himself master of this important fortress, established his winter quarters in Bohemia, and driven the remnants of Browne and of Piccolomini across the Danube, or at least beyond the mountains of that kingdom. As a result of these two mistakes, his forces were inferior to those of the enemy at the battlefield of Lobositz, although in the general field of operations he outnumbered his enemy three to one. He was also forced to take his winter quarters in Saxony and Silesia. No doubt he won great advantages from this campaign, but he could have obtained greater advantages still.

First Campaign of 1757

I. The campaign of 1757 began on 15 April, was terminated on 15 December, and lasted 240 days. It is divided into two periods, the first comprising the marches, maneuvers, and engagements from 15 April to 15 July, and the second those actions from 15 July until 15 December. In the first period Frederick fought two major battles—Prague, which he won on 4 May, and Kolin, which he lost on 18 June.

During the previous year neither France, Sweden, Russia, nor the Holy Roman Empire had put an army into the field, but instead devoted the entire time to preparations and demonstrations. The same was true of the first phase of the campaign of 1757, when Frederick had only to deal with Austrian armies. The Prussian army was better drilled, more numerous, and was composed of veteran troops. At the beginning of April it was organized into four corps: the First under the orders of Prince Maurice of Anhalt-Dessau, located at Chemnitz; the Second, commanded by Frederick himself, at the village of Loschwitz, near Dresden; the Third, under the Prince of Bevern, at Zittau in Lusatia; and the Fourth, under Marshal Schwerin, at Silesia.[1]

The Austrian army, commanded by Marshal Browne, was in Bohemia. The Duke of Arenberg, with the First Corps, constituted the left at Egra; Marshal Browne, with the Second Corps, was at the camp of Budin, in front of Prague. The Third Corps, commanded by the Count of Koenigsegg, was at Reichenberg, and the Fourth Corps, under the orders of General Daun, was in Moravia. The four Prussian army corps comprised 100,000 men under arms, of which some 65,000 or 66,000 were infantry, 16,000 to 18,000 were cavalry, and the rest were artillery, sappers, miners, etc., forming 108 battalions and 160 squadrons, not counting twenty-six battalions and sixty squadrons then assembling in Pomerania to contain the

Russians. The four Austrian armies were smaller, much inferior in quality, and they lacked many things.

Frederick resolved to benefit from the four months' start he had over the Russians by striking a sudden blow and placing himself in a position to comfort the other armies as they arrived into line. He invaded Bohemia and besieged Prague, thus executing in this campaign what he had been unable to accomplish during the preceding one.

II. The corps of Prince Maurice, which constituted the right of the Prussian line, began to maneuver in April, threatening Egra and advancing in two columns by Kommotau on the Eger. For his part, Frederick crossed the mountains at Peterswald and arrived on the Eger, at Lobositz, and on 23 April he crossed the river at Loschwitz, at the head of his two united corps. Marshal Browne, who had been joined at his camp at Budin, behind the Eger, by the Duke of Arenberg, fell back to the camp at Prague as soon as the King had crossed the Eger. The Prussian army followed him, arriving before Prague on 21 May. But already Prince Charles of Lorraine, who had taken command of the imperial army, was encamped on the heights of Ziska, on the right bank of the Moldau.

The Prince of Bevern crossed the mountain between Zittau and Reichenberg, where he was stopped by the excellent position occupied by Count of Koenigsegg, who forced him to maneuver for several days before he could dislodge the Austrians, which he accomplished only after a stubborn combat. The Count of Koenigsegg fell back to Liebenau, where he occupied a position every bit as formidable.

Meanwhile Marshal Schwerin, proceding from Silesia and having found no enemy force in front of him, debouched into Bohemia at Trautenau and moved to Jung-Bunzlau, in the rear of the Count of Koenigsegg's position, forcing the latter to abandon his position and recross the Elbe to move on Prague, where he joined the Prince of Lorraine. Schwerin, at the head of his corps and that of Duke Bevern, followed this movement and on 4 May he encamped on the right bank of the Elbe, at Alt-Bunzlau, opposite Brandis. Since the enemy did not occupy the opposite bank, he sent a vanguard there.

The Prince of Lorraine waited for several days for General Daun, who was bringing reinforcements of 30,000 men from Moravia, which would have equalized the two armies.

Frederick perceived the full importance of preventing this junction. On 5 May, at daybreak, he constructed a bridge about four or five miles below Prague, at the village of Podbaba, without encountering any resistance—even though he was within about 4,000 yards of the Austrian camp—and established himself with twenty battalions and thirty-eight squadrons at Cimic, on the right bank of the Moldau. Marshal Schwerin crossed the Elbe and advanced to Mieschitz. The two Prussian armies during this night were no more than nine miles apart. On the sixth, at daybreak, they made their junction at the village of Prosek.

Frederick's army formed its order of battle, his right at Prosek, the center in front of Gabel, and the left beyond Satalic, occupying a series of hills extending over four miles, and being mounted on the Brandis road, which was his line of operation. The Prince of Lorraine had his left on the Ziska, near the Moldau, and his right on the heights of the village of Key, forming a line 9,000 yards in length. The King had on the battlefield sixty-four battalions of infantry and 123 squadrons of cavalry, roughly 60,000 men. Marshal Keith had remained on the left bank of the Moldau before Prague, with twenty-six battalions of infantry and twenty-six squadrons of cavalry. Nine battalions and eleven squadrons were detached on the double line of operation to cover the magazines.

The Prince of Lorraine had nearly 70,000 men, but 10,000 had remained in Prague to defend the city and observe Marshal Keith.

The two armies thus found themselves equal in number on the battlefield. The Austrian army established its left near the Moldau, where the Prussian army had posted its right. The two armies were about 6,000 yards apart, separated by a deep valley through which flowed a stream formed by the discharging from several ponds, marshy and with steep banks. The source of the stream was above the pond of Sterbohol, some 12,000 to 14,000 yards from Prague, where it turns and passes by the villages of Sterbohol, Pocernic, Hostawiic, Hrdlorz, and Hiaupetin, and flows into the Moldau near Liben, some 4,000 yards below Prague.

Convinced that this stream would effectively protect the front of the enemy army, Frederick directed a march by the left to outflank it. The Prince of Lorraine noticed the movement in sufficient time to order the infantry on his right to change front to the rear, thus placing it at right angles at the end of the center, and supporting itself on the heights of Sterbohol, constituting an angle of 3,000 yards, which he prolonged by 4,000 additional yards by sending the cavalry on his left to extend it. . . . His line thus occupied two sides of a right angle, one perpendicular and the other parallel to Prague, each side being more than 6,000 to 7,000 yards in length.

Frederick halted his troops as soon as his extreme right had reached the heights of Key, with his center being opposite Pocernic and his left in front of Sterbohol. He sent the cavalry of his reserve to reinforce Schwerin's cavalry in the plain of Sterbohol. This movement uncovered his line of operation, the Brandis–Gabel road, and the Prussian army found itself astride the road from Kolin, by which General Daun arrived the same day at Boehmisch-Brod, eight leagues from the battlefield.

The Austrian infantry, beyond the stream that covered its front and nearly 2,000 yards from the half-square, occupied positions commanding the village of Gabel. Frederick had these detached posts attacked and overthrown while Marshal Schwerin, with the left wing, crossed the stream at Sterbohol and Pocernic, the cavalry in the villages, the artillery on the dikes, and the infantry in the marshes. He encountered great difficulties: several regiments sank down to their knees. The Austrian right failed to take advantage of this, remaining on the hills to rectify its alignment.

At one o'clock in the afternoon Schwerin attacked with the bayonet, advancing as far as the enemy's position. Overwhelmed however by grapeshot, his troops gave way and abandoned the heights. Brown pursued them for about 2,400 to 3,000 yards. The left and center of the Austrian army remained unshaken. The Prussian cavalry debouched into the plain of Sterbohol, made an unsuccessful attack but rallied, returned to the fight and routed the Austrian cavalry, driving it from the battlefield. The Prince of Lorraine's right flank thus found itself entirely uncovered at the moment when Frederick himself entered the village of Key and attacked his left flank. The Prince of Bevern, who marched to the center, noticed a gap at the angle of the two lines, threw himself into it and got involved in the most stubborn fight.

Meanwhile Marshal Schwerin, having rallied his infantry, returned to the combat. Although he was mortally wounded while leading his regiment, his troops continued the attack against the Austrian right, which, taken in flank by the King and overwhelmed by the cavalry, gave ground and was routed, thus deciding the day.

The Prince of Lorraine abandoned all of his positions. He supported his retreat by the troops of his center and left who had not given way. However, constantly outflanked on his right, 12,000 of his men were cut off at Prague and only with difficulty succeeded in making their way to Marshal Daun's camp.

The Austrians lost 16,000 men and 200 guns and Marshal Browne was mortally wounded. The Prussians lost 12,000 men.

III. This battle cost the Prince of Lorraine's army 30,000 men. Although he still had 40,000 soldiers, their morale was affected. Frederick invested Prague on the two banks of the Moldau. Since this fortress had a circumference of 14,000 yards, Frederick's line of contravallation was 30,000 yards in length, its barracks being separated by a large river.

In vain he hoped that the lack of provisions would promptly force his enemy to capitulate. Instead the blockade lasted six weeks, until 18 June, when Frederick was forced to raise the siege as a consequence of the battle of Kolin.

On 7 May Marshal Daun learned of the disasters of the Prince of Lorraine. For several days he remained at Boehmisch-Brod to gather up the debris of his army and, after having rallied the 12,000 men who had not been able to enter Prague, he fell back some twenty-eight miles and encamped under the walls of Kolin. When Frederick ordered Prince Bevern to follow him with a body of 25,000 troops, Daun continued his retreat as far as Goltsch-Jenikau, two miles in front of Habern and fory-eight miles from Prague.

On 12 June Daun, having received reinforcements, moved back to the village of Krichnau, within two miles of Kolin, where he encamped, his left at Swojsic and the right at Chocenic, having in front of him the road from Prague to Kolin.

Now it was Bevern's turn to retreat. Frederick moved in great haste from the camp at Prague with reinforcements, bringing his headquarters on the 14th to the small village of Kaurzim, six miles from Krichnau. Here he encamped, his left supported by the road from Prague to Kolin, at the village of Planian, drawing provisions from Nimburg, a small village on the left of the Elbe, ten miles distant. He remained there the 15th and a part of the 16th to allow time for his reinforcements and his caissons of provisions to arrive.

On the 16th, as Frederick was about to begin his march to move to the position at Swojsic to contain Daun, whom he believed to be at Kohl-Janowic, he learned that this marshal instead was at Krichnau. Now he could execute his projected movement only by passing his corps on the way.

On the 17th Frederick marched by his left and encamped on both sides of the road from Prague, with Planian in front of him and Kolin six miles farther on. He thus found himself encamped at right angles to the left of the Austrian army.

At daybreak on the 18th he began his march, left wing in front, the vanguard under General Zieten, fifty-five squadrons and seven battalions strong, at the head. The army marched in three lines: the first, comprising only infantry, followed the road from Prague to Kolin. The other two, farther on the left, marched between the road and the Elbe.

General Daun had made some movements during the night. At daybreak the Prussians could see only a few vedettes, but as soon as they had passed Planian they saw the Austrian army drawn up in line of battle. This caused the Prussians to halt. The advance guard had reached the height of Zlatislunz, 6,000 yards in front of Planian. The main body was at Novimiesto and Planian. The Austrian army was formed with its left at Brezan, the center at Chocenic, and the right at Krechor. It thus occupied a curved bow of 7,000 yards, the right beside Kolin and the left on the side of Prague, enveloping the road from Prague to Kolin, which was the bowstring.

The Austrians were arrayed in several lines: the second occupied the crest of the heights and the first was slightly sloped, having in its front three fortified villages filled with infantry and covered by artillery. The left found itself 1,000 yards from the main road from Planian to Kolin, on which the Prussian army was marching. The center, or the village of Chocenic, was 2,000 yards from the road, and the right, or the village of Krechor, was distant 1,000 yards. Thus the two armies were near to one another and in a bizarre formation. Frederick found himself outflanking the entire enemy left, while the enemy line formed a semicircle, of which the diameter or chord was a part of the road from Planian to Kolin—which Frederick occupied.

At one hour past noon Frederick ordered his troops to continue the march, thus moving along the chord of a semicircle on which the Austrian army occupied higher ground. He could do this only by defiling under fire of musketry and cannon. General Nádasdy, commanding the Austrian cavalry, rode immediately to within 4,000 yards of Kolin, mounted on the road, thus obstructing Kolin to the Prussians and forcing them to remain under fire of his army. Daun ordered all of his troops to advance to the extremity of the position and fired a hail of bullets, balls, and shells into the marching columns. The skirmishers of the troops posted in the villages moved forward. Firing broke out between the Croats and the Prussian army, which nevertheless endeavored to continue its movement.

The Prussian advance guard, being in front, succeeded in crossing the 6,000 yards to outflank the Austrian right. After having gone beyond Krechor, it faced to the right, marched on the extreme right and seized the village of Krechor. But the Prussian army was so heavily engaged and the firing was so lively that it was forced to halt, form on the right into line, and march forward at a cadence of 140 steps a minute to drive back the skirmishers. The latter were supported and the Prussians made futile efforts to seize the heights, which at the same time were attacked on their right.

The Austrians, however, enjoyed every advantage of position. The Prussian attack was an affair of unforeseen circumstances. They had to scale the steep mountains and cross footpaths and impassable ravines. They performed prodigies of valor, but, forced to give way, they lost their artillery, a large number of prisoners, and a great many killed and wounded. They fell back on Planian and made their retreat to Nimburg. Marshal Daun returned to his camp, where he remained several days chanting Te Deums. The Prussian losses amounted to 15,000, the Austrians lost 5,000. Thus, for every two men in his army Frederick had lost one *hors de combat*.

On the 19th Frederick raised the siege of Prague and returned to Brandis, where the artillery was transported in order to be embarked on the Elbe. Since it had only eight miles to go, it arrived on the same evening, the 19th. Marshal Keith, who was on the left bank, remained twenty-four hours longer and then retreated to Leitmeritz, where he crossed the Elbe. Actively pursued, he lost 400 or 500 men.

Frederick then divided his army into two bodies, both of them on the right bank of the Elbe. He camped near Leitmeritz with most of his troops, sending the Prince Royal of Prussia with the remainder, first behind the Iser, at Cejtic, and then to Boehmisch-Leipa, behind the Polzen, where he found himself thus extended twenty miles from Frederick and twelve or fourteen miles distant from his magazines at Zittau.

The Prince of Lorraine finally left Prague on 1 July, crossed the Elbe near Brandis to Celakowic, moved on Munchengraetz, behind the Iser, thence to Huhnerwasser, turned the position of the Prince Royal at Boehmisch-Leipa, seized Niemen and Gabel, and thus intercepted the communication with Zittau, which the Prince Royal could reach only by a circuitous route and after having burned his caissons. He arrived there on the 22nd, slightly in advance of the Austrian army, which bombarded Zittau in the presence of the Prussians. A portion of the magazines was burned. The Prince of Prussia retreated to Bautzen by way of Loebau.

On 29 July Frederick left his camp at Leitmeritz and joined the camp at Bautzen, and several days later he encamped at Bernstadt, between Loebau and Goerlitz. The Prince of Lorraine was encamped in front of Zittau, keeping a garrison in Goerlitz and thus intercepting the road from Silesia.

During the night of 15 August Frederick moved to Hirschfelde, between Zittau and Goerlitz, thus cutting the Prince of Lorraine off from the fortress at Zittau. He took possession of Goerlitz, reconnoitered the Prince of Lorraine's camp, which he judged to be unassailable, and, seeing that this prince refused combat, he returned to Hirschfelde, leaving the command of the army to the Prince of Bevern. On 24 August he marched for the Saale with a detachment of sixteen battalions and thirty squadrons. Thus ended the first period of this campaign.

Third Observation. Frederick's plan to make himself master of Prague and Bohemia was good in 1756; it was still feasible at the beginning of 1757. There, as if it were a great intrenched camp, he might have covered Saxony and Silesia and contained Austria and the Holy Roman Empire. He was bound to have succeeded in this enterprise—all of the odds were in his favor. He possessed the initiative of movement and his troops were superior both in number and quality, to say nothing of his own audacity and great talents. Yet he failed.

I. He marched to the conquest of Bohemia by two lines of operation, with two armies separated from each other by 120 miles. These had to join each other eighty miles from the point of departure, under the walls of a fortress and in the presence of enemy armies. It is a principle that the union of separate army corps must never take place near the enemy.

Yet Frederick was successful. His two armies, although separated by mountains and defiles, surmounted all obstacles without experiencing any disaster. By 4 May they were only twelve miles apart but still were separated by two rivers, the fortress of Prague, and the Prince of Lorraine's army, 70,000 strong. Their junction would seem impossible, yet it was achieved by daybreak on 6 May, within 600 yards of the Austrian camp. Fortune must have heaped full measure upon Frederick, who should have been defeated in detail before the two columns reunited, and each driven separately out of Bohemia.

II. Since Frederick abandoned his line of operation by the left bank of the Elbe and took a line of operation by Brandis and the right bank, he should have made Marshal Keith cross to the right bank of the Moldau and remain his extreme right, covering in any event his line of operation on Brandis. This would have given him three advantages:

(a) His entire army would have been united, and he would have had nothing to fear from the enterprises of the Prince of Lorraine.

(b) He would have had 20,000 more men on the battlefield at Prague, an immense advantage, and

(c) His line of operation on Brandis would have always been secure. It would not have been compromised, as in fact it was.

III. During the battle of Prague the King abandoned the road from Brandis, his line of operation and of retreat, and placed himself astride the road from Kolin, then occupied by Marshal Daun fifteen miles in the rear. If the Prince of Lorraine could have presented his left and occupied Gabel while Marshal Daun approached, Frederick would have been surrounded.

Fourth Observation.

I. The Prince of Lorraine permitted Frederick to arrive in front of Prague and Marshal Schwerin to reach Brandis, twelve miles apart, without having taken advantage of the opportunity to march to encounter Schwerin on the right bank of the Elbe and, joining the Count of Koenigsegg, to overwhelm him with twice his force while Frederick was measuring the ramparts of Prague. Nor did he endeavor to attack and defeat Frederick, after being joined by the Count of Koenigsegg, while Schwerin, still on the right bank of the Elbe, was separated from Frederick by the Moldau and the Elbe.

II. Marshal Daun needed two days before he could reach the camp at Prague, which would have increased his army to 100,000 men, and he did not conceive the possibility of gaining this time by defending the Moldau against Frederick, who crossed it 4,000 yards from his camp, or by disputing Schwerin's passage of the Elbe, which he accomplished eight miles from his camp.

III. After Frederick had crossed the Moldau, during the night of the fifth, the Prince of Lorraine should have returned to Prague at seven o'clock that evening, leaving 15,000 men in his position at Ziska to mask his movement, and reaching the King's bridge at daybreak, to burn the bridge and attack and rout Marshal Keith, pursuing him with 100 squadrons, and returning to Prague that evening. Marshal Daun would have approached, and by the 7th they would have attacked together had Frederick waited for him.

IV. The Prince was defeated because he had deployed his army without skill. He should have placed his left where his center was, his center where his right was located, and his right where he stationed a portion of the cavalry. His infantry then would have been well supported and his cavalry would have been near the pond of Sterbohol. He should have kept a third of his cavalry and a sixth of his infantry in reserve. And finally, having committed the mistake of paralyzing his left, he should have brought it back into action by ordering it to march to the aid of the troops on the height near Gabel, which would have instantly stopped Frederick's movement. Frederick then would have been outflanked on his right, which was "in the air."

Fifth Observation.

I. Frederick's plan to surround a town the size of Prague, containing an army of 40,000 men (which, it is true, had just lost a battle), is one of the most daring and comprehensive that has ever been conceived in modern times. He used 50,000 men for this blockade, but he had reason to fear that the blockade would be disturbed by Marshal Daun's army. He should have taken advantage of the six weeks that he had left to establish strong lines of circumvallation and contravallation, formed an army of observation and placed it in suitable positions twenty or twenty-five miles to his rear and intrenching it there; and as soon as Marshal Daun approached to raise the siege, he should have reinforced his army of observation with a portion of the blockading army and defeated Daun before the besieged army was aware of it. But Frederick did nothing during the six weeks that elapsed before Marshal Daun was able to advance.

II. His plan of taking position under Kolin, some twenty-eight miles from Prague, separated him by more than a full day's march from a portion of the blockading army, and vice versa.

III. At the battle of Kolin it is difficult to justify his attempt to turn Daun's right by making a flank march of 6,000 yards within 10,000 yards from the heights occupied by the enemy's army. This was so rash an operation, so contrary to the principles of war. "Never make a flank march in front of an army in position, particularly if it occupies heights that dominate the terrain where you must defile." Had he attacked the left flank of the Austrian army he would have been perfectly placed for that, but to march in front of an entire army occupying the highest ground, under fire of grapeshot and musketry, and to outflank an opposing wing is to assume that the opposing army has neither cannon nor muskets.

Some Prussian writers have claimed that his maneuver failed only because of the impatience of a battalion commander who, tired of the fire of the Austrian skirmishers, gave the command "the right into line," and in so doing engaged the entire column. That is inaccurate. Frederick was present; all of the generals were aware of his plans, and it was not 4,000 yards from the head to the rear of the column. The movement made by the Prussian army was governed by the greatest of interests—the need for self-preservation and the instinct of every man not to be killed without defending himself.

Sixth Observation. The fact that the Prince of Lorraine had been cooped up in Prague for the first ten days must be regarded as the result of the battle. However, once he perceived that Frederick had made a strong detachment against Marshal Daun and that the morale of his army had been restored, his lack of activity is criminal. At daybreak he should have attacked one fourth of the enemy with his entire force, defeated him, and immediately fallen back into the fortress, and performed the same maneuver several times against other points, thus destroying the Prussian army in detail. What would have kept him from moving at nightfall against both the height of Tiska and corresponding heights at the salient part of the Prague bastion, constructing ten or twelve redoubts during the night, and forming at daybreak into a line of battle 3,000 yards long, which he might have covered with artillery? He could have used every day after that to fortify his camp or to occupy and fortify positions that could have increased its extent and made it more offensive. In that way he could have greatly embarrassed his enemy and would have been informed of all of Marshal Daun's movements until the moment when, judging that his approach must draw off a portion of Frederick's force, he would have forced him to raise the siege. In his situation he ought to have fought every day alternatively on the two banks.

Seventh Observation. The conduct of Marshal Daun, which one assumes to have been based upon the resources that he knew existed in Prague, would appear to have been good until after the battle of Kolin, but he is guilty of not having profited from his victory. He might just as well have not won the battle. After a dozen days of deliberation he finally decided to move into Lusatia. It would have been more in keeping with the spirit of this war had he marched instead into Saxony. He could have retaken Dresden and rallied the army of the Prince of Soubise and perhaps also that of the Duke de Richelieu, the Swedes, and the Russians. He would have assembled 200,000 men at Berlin.

The Austrian generals in this campaign were extremely timid. Although their troops had fought courageously, the general had demonstrated no confidence in them. They could have attacked the Prince of Prussia at Zittau, but they did not. The King constantly offered them battle after Kolin, and constantly they avoided it.

Second Campaign of 1757

I. This second epoch of the campaign of 1757 begins on 15 July and ends on 15 December. Lasting 150 days, it is fertile with great results. On 26 July the French won the battle of Hastenbeck; on 5 November they lost at Rossbach; the Prussians lost the battle of Jaegerndorf against the Russians on 31 August, and the battle of Breslau on 24 November.

But Frederick won immortality and redeemed everything by winning the battle of Leuthen on 5 December. He had nearly 120,000 men in the field in this second period, not counting the garrisons of his fortresses. He faced 180,000 men from different nations, acting isolated and without harmony. The management and quality of the troops were on his side. One can understand, therefore, when the campaign ended to his advantage.

The three enemy armies were: first, 50,000 men maneuvering on the Saale, commanded by the Prince of Soubise and the Duke of Hildburghausen, half of them French and the rest contingents from the empire, very poor troops; second, 60,000 Russians, who arrived in August, fought one battle and then returned home; and third, the army of the Prince of Lorraine, 80,000 strong, which operated in Silesia. Among these belligerent armies we do not include either the army of Marshal d'Estrées, 80,000 strong, nor the army of the Duke of Cumberland, which was opposed to it.

II. The Court of Versailles had pledged to furnish 24,000 men to the Queen of Hungary. The Prince of Soubise took command of these, crossed the Rhine at Düsseldorf, and moved into Saxony, where he joined the army of the contingents of the Holy Roman Empire. He entered Erfurt on 21 August.

France, being at war with England, wanted to seize Hanover. An army of 80,000 men, composed of 112 battalions and ten squadrons, under the command of the Marshal d'Estrées, having as lieutenant generals MM. de Chevert, d'Armentières, and Contades, crossed the Rhine, penetrated into Westphalia, and marched toward the Weser. The Duke of Cumberland occupied the camp at Bielefeld with Hanoverian, Hessian, and Brunswick contingents—60,000 men in the pay of England. Upon the approach of the French he recrossed the Weser, and on 22 June camped at Hastenbeck, the right resting on the Weser, covered by a marsh; the center at Hastenbeck, and the left on the heights of Hohnsen, three or four miles in front of the fortresss of Hameln. He occupied a line 5,000 yards in extent.

On 16 July Marshal d'Estrées crossed the Weser above the fortress of Hameln in six columns. On the 24th he took up a position in front of the enemy army, saw that the enemy's position could not be attacked by way of the heights on the left, and detached Chevert, who on the 25th, with sixteen battalions, turned the enemy's left and took position in the village of Afferde, in their rear. The general, with twenty-four infantry battalions and four regiments of dragoons, occupied an intermediate position.

On the 26th Chevert, supported by d'Armentières, attacked the extreme left of the Duke of Cambridge. At the same time the French left, led by Marshal d'Estrées himself, appeared before the Hanoverian center and right at Hastenbeck, but it could not reach that place until five in the evening. Chevert was already master of the heights and had dislodged the elite of the enemy army. The retreat of the Duke of Cumberland had become difficult when the Hereditary Prince of Brunswick, with 1,200 of his troops supported by a Hanoverian regiment, penetrated through some woods to the center of Chevert's troops, who initially were thrown into confusion and abandoned several guns. A party of several hundred cavalry having made its appearance in the rear of the French army, Marshal d'Estrées in alarm ordered a retreat, but Chevert's troops recovered from their astonishment, perceived quickly how few men the Duke of Brunswick had, and recaptured their artillery. However, during this confusion the Duke of Cumberland made good his retreat, saving his artillery. He suffered few losses. The battlefield and the victory went to the French. The loss on both sides was about 3,000 men.

Several days later Marshal d'Estrées was replaced by the Duke de Richelieu, who, on 9 September, signed a convention with the Duke of Cumberland at Kloster-Zeven. The entire electorate was occupied by the French army. The troops from Brunswick and Hesse returned to their countries without either being disarmed or made prisoners of war. The Hanoverians went into cantonments.

Several weeks later the Duke de Richelieu moved his headquarters to Halberstadt.

Frederick, however, alarmed by the arrival on the Saale of the Prince of Soubise and the Duke of Hildburghausen, had departed . . . from his camp at Bernstadt on 24 August with sixteen battalions and twenty-three squadrons, leaving the Duke de Bevern with fifty-six battalions and 100 squadrons for the defense of Silesia. He was joined en route by Prince Maurice, with twenty battalions and twenty squadrons. Upon his approach, Soubise fell back to Eisenach. Frederick followed him to Gotha, which he entered on 15 September. From there he fell back on Leipzig, leaving [General] Seydlitz at Gotha with fifteen squadrons as a corps of observation.

The King having been forced to approach the Elbe to relieve Berlin, Seydlitz evacuated Gotha and took position halfway between Gotha and Erfurt. Soubise immediately moved himself to Gotha with all of his headquarters, 8,000 grenadiers, and a division of cavalry, but no sooner had he set up there when Seydlitz, placing his fifteen squadrons in a single rank, marched boldly against enemy headquarters, which made good its escape in great haste to Eisenach. The 8,000 grenadiers made good their retreat after firing several musket rounds. The headquarters baggage and some prisoners fell into the hands of the Prussians. This disgraceful episode was the prelude to Rossbach.

Seeing that the combined armies of France and the empire refused any combat, the Prussian King moved his headquarters to Buttstaedt, where he remained until 10 October. However, Hadik's quartermaster general, with a body of Austrian partisans, had entered Berlin on 16 October and had laid it under contribution. This news stimulated activity on the part of Soubise, who took up his march on the 27th, crossed the Saale, and moved his headquarters to Weissenfels. Frederick returned as soon as he heard the news, reunited his different detachments, and with 25,000 men marched to Weissenfels. On the 29th the French evacuated upon his approach and recrossed the Saale. On 2 November the King crossed the river on the three bridges at Weissenfels, Merseburg, and Halle. Upon learning this the allies reunited themselves in a single camp.

III. On 3 November Frederick set out to attack them but, arriving within musket range of their camp, he noticed that they had changed position. He withdrew by his left and encamped, his right at Breda, center at Schortau, and left at Rossbach. Emboldened by this withdrawal, the allies in turn decided to attack, and conceived a plan that would turn Frederick's left flank, since his right and center struck them as being too strongly posted. On the 5th they executed this movement in three columns and without an advance guard. They outflanked the left of the Prussian army by going from 2,400 to 3,000 yards, intercepting the road from Weissenfels and seizing the road from Merseburg.

The King, who had been observing them for two hours, had made his dispositions to attack them on their flank and the head of their column, taking advantage of some hills that masked his movement. General Seydlitz, with all the cavalry and several batteries of light artillery, moved on the extreme left, to the right of Lunstaedt. Prince Henry, with one brigade of six battalions, drew up in battle array on his right. The entire army followed. The tail of the column was still at Rossbach, which then became the extreme right of the Prussian army.

The Prussian army had thus made a change of front to the rear, the right in front. The allied army, having no advance guard, was smashed in by the charges of the Prussian cavalry and by the fire of many guns. The French and Allied cavalry were driven back upon the infantry, the disorder being spread throughout the entire army. In a few hours the victory belonged to the Prussians, who had fought with only six battalions, had suffered 300 casualties, and had captured 7,000 prisoners, twenty-seven colors, and a large number of cannon. This makeshift allied army, in the greatest disorder, managed to rally beyond the Thuringian mountains.

IV. Russia had put in motion an army of 60,000 men, which crossed Poland in four columns. The right column, commanded by General Fermor, invested Memel, assisted by a squadron of nine warships under the orders of Admiral Lewis. Memel capitulated on 6 August.

Marshal Apraxin was commander in chief. He crossed the Niemen, the Pregel, and took up a position. Prussian Marshal Lehwaldt, who was camped at Insterburg with 30,000 men, marched to meet the Russians and on 29 August camped opposite their position at the village of Jaegerndorf. The following day, the 30th, the Prussians, despite inferior numbers, marched against the enemy. They maneuvered in the oblique order to turn the Russian left, and after a stubborn battle they were defeated. Marshal Lehwaldt fell back to Wehlau. The Russians suffered 5,000 casualties, the Prussians 3,000. Several days later, on 22 December, the Russian general, although victorious, fell back across the Pregel and the Niemen and reentered his own country, abandoning his conquests with the exception of Memel. The Prussian general, no longer having an enemy before him, returned to the Oder.

Fifteen thousand Swedes had landed in Pomerania and seized Anklam and the islands of Usedom and Wollin. They were observed only by the garrison of Stettin, but, upon the arrival of Marshal Lehwaldt, they were driven into Stralsund during the first days of December.

V. Several days after the King had left Silesia, the Duke of Bevern abandoned his camp at Bernstadt and took position on the mountain of Landeskrone, near Goerlitz, keeping one division camped at Bautzen. The Prince of Lorraine, who occupied the camp of Bernstadt, sent General Nádasdy to the Neisse to secure a bridge and dislodge the enemy division of Bautzen, cutting all of its communications with Saxony. On 7 September he occupied Holtzberg.

The Duke of Bevern crossed the Neisse and marched by way of Naumburg, Bunzlau, Haynau, and Liegnitz, to the Oder, where he arrived on 9 September.

The Prince of Lorraine followed him in a parallel direction by way of Lauban, Loewenberg, Goldberg, Jauer, and Neudorf, where he encamped on the 26th. The following day the Duke of Bevern moved to Glogau, where he crossed the Oder and marched upon Breslau along the right bank, and on 1 October camped on the banks of the Lohe, covering Breslau. The Prince of Lorraine invested Schweidnitz, opening the trenches on 27 October. On 11 November he took three of the forts by assault. The governor capitulated and surrendered himself and 6,000 men as prisoners.

Encouraged by this conquest, the Prince of Lorraine resolved to attack the Duke of Bevern in his intrenched camp before Breslau. Bevern's right rested on the Oder, at the village of Kosel, and his left was at Klein-Mochbern, on a fine fortified plateau. The Lohe covered his front; he occupied the villages of Pilsnitz and Schmiedefeld as bridgeheads, and by his right he communicated with the suburb of St. Nichols of Breslau. His army was 36,000 to 40,000 strong.

On the opposite bank the Prince of Lorraine held parallel position between Strachwitz and Masselwitz. Both armies were fortified in these positions. After the surrender of Schweidnitz, Nádasdy rejoined his army and moved to the right, threatening to march on Breslau, outflanking the entire left of the Prussian camp. General Zieten, with seven battalions and fifty squadrons, was detached to the left to oppose this movement.

On 22 November the Austrian army took up arms at daybreak and made three assaults against the Lohe while simultaneously outflanking the Prussian left. By midday it had thrown seven bridges across this river. The attack then became very lively. All of Nádasdy's efforts on the right did not force Zieten to give ground, but the Prince of Lorraine did sieze the position of Klein-Mochbern. The Prussian army lost its battlefield and found itself driven under the walls of Breslau. The Prussians estimated their loss at 6,000 men, not counting the 10,000 that were captured in Breslau. The Austrian loss was 4,000 men.

The day after the battle the Duke of Bevern was taken prisoner during a reconnaissance, and Zieten assumed command of the Prussian army, which recrossed the Oder with what was left of its troops, descended the left bank, and proceeded to Glogau, where it met Frederick, who had returned from Saxony and who, after leaving Leipzig on 12 November with eighteen battalions and twenty-one squadrons, reached Parchwitz on the 28th, where the junction was made on 3 December. As a consequence of the battle of Breslau there were a great many deserters in the Prussian army, and Frederick could unite only 36,000 men at the camp at Parchwitz. The Austrian forces were estimated at twice that number.

On December 4, at daybreak, the Prussian army marched on Neumarkt, where the advance guard routed a body of 4,000 Croats and took hundreds of prisoners. The Prince of Lorraine had left Breslau to move forward and had encamped on the left bank of the river at Schweidnitz, his center at the village of Leuthen, his right in the woods of Nippern, and his left at a strong position resting on the river.

The next day, 5 December, the Prussian advance guard marched to Borne and captured 600 prisoners. The army followed in four columns, filing before the enemy's front through a marshy valley, protected in its movement by fog and hills. It concealed its march from the enemy and moved against his extreme left, which it threw into disorder. All efforts on the part of the Austrian generals to draw up the left in battle array were of no avail: the Prussians arrived everywhere before the troops were formed. Marshal Daun, seeing their continuous progress on his left, marched forward with his right, which he personally commanded. However, his troops were attacked and overwhelmed by the cavalry. The debris of the Austrian army recrossed the Schweidnitz and tried to rally on the opposite bank.

This army lost 6,500 men, killed or wounded, 7,000 prisoners, and 150 guns. The Prussian army lost 2,000 men. The Prince of Lorraine evacuated Breslau, leaving behind 20,000 sick, wounded, and stragglers, which fell into the hands of the victor, and retreated in great haste into Bohemia. Both armies then went into winter quarters.

Eighth Observation.

I. Marshal d'Estrées took three months to cross the Rhine at Weser. With an army one third larger than the enemy and consisting of Frenchmen, he barely won the victory at Hastenbeck over an army formed of troops of six different princes. This testifies to the sorry composition of the French staff at the time.

II. Chevert's movement made on the eve of the battle was dangerous and contrary to the principles. If it produced no adverse effects it was only because Marshal d'Estrées enjoyed a great superiority over the enemy.

III. The attack of Chevert and d'Armentières on the day of the battle was well conceived and would have been sufficient to provide decisive victory had it been supported by sixty squadrons of cavalry, useless no doubt for attacking against heights but necessary in order to descend them, pursue the enemy, and decide the victory.

IV. The moral effect produced by the Duke of Brunswick, with 1,200 men, gained time for the Duke of Cumberland to secure his retreat, and to decide the outcome of the battle. It demonstrates the lack of experience of the French officers, yet Chevert was there.

V. Marshal d'Estrées inappropriately ordered the retreat. The attack of the Hereditary Prince and the part of cavalry that appeared on his line of communication were entirely isolated incidents that could have had no connection with each other. His imagination, however, took over and gave him a false picture of conditions. He thought that he had detected signs of a plan that the enemy was about to execute that would place him in danger, and he let his imagination influence his judgment. The attack of the Hereditary Prince had only begun.

He should have been patient, let events decide, and waited until everything was unmasked. Besides, what could the marshal have to fear? Chevert had enough troops to repulse the entire army of the Duke of Cumberland. The hussars appearing in his rear could be of no great danger except to the sutlers. At the very most he should have been content to send a light cavalry brigade to repulse them.

The foremost quality of a general in chief is to keep a cool head, receiving accurate impressions from objects, and never yielding to overexcitement or being dazzled or intoxicated by good or bad news; a mind that classifies the successive or simultaneous sensations it receives throughout the course of a day, so that these can be seen in the proper context; for common sense and reason are the outgrowth of the comparison of several sensations taken into equal consideration.

VI. The Convention of Kloster-Zeven makes no sense. The Duke of Cumberland was done for. He was forced to lay down his arms and become a prisoner. It therefore was not possible to consent to any other term of capitulation than that.

The Duke de Richelieu was wrong not to disarm and disband the Hanoverian troops.

VII. The scuffle at Gotha, where an entire headquarters, protected by one division of 8,000 grenadiers and several thousand cavalrymen, allowed themselves to be frightened and to run away before 1,500 hussars, without looking behind them, describes sufficiently what one should expect from a general of such a weak character as the Prince of Soubise and the Duke of Hildburghausen.

VIII. The result of the battle of Rossbach is not unusual: 22,000 to 26,000 Prussians, elite troops and well commanded, ought to have defeated 45,000 to 50,000 men composed of troops from the empire that were so poorly commanded at this time. But what has been a matter of astonishment and disgrace is to have been defeated by six battalions and thirty squadrons! It is not for an army composed of such troops and commanded by such officers—whose spirit and intellect were so weak and whose resources were so sluggish—to undertake a flank march across the front of such a well-established army.

IX. Frederick's maneuver is natural and deserves less praise than the enemy deserves blame, for it was forced upon him by this imprudent march, made without being either protected by a corps of observation in position or reconnoitered by some flankers and an advance guard, in order to be safe from any surprise in hilly country and hazy weather.

Ninth Observation. The Duke of Bevern's position at the battle of Breslau is faulty, in that it did not cover Breslau. This general had fortified positions on the right of the city, and had the Prince of Lorraine maneuvered better, he could not have fired a single musket shot before these intrenchments. He could have pushed his right under Nádasdy still closer to the Oder, thus enabling him to completely turn the intrenched camp and change his line of operation, abandoning that from Schweidnitz in favor of one from Upper Silesia. The Prussian general had no interest in fighting a battle, since he awaited Frederick with reinforcements. It was therefore essentially a question of defending a camp that covered Breslau. It is difficult to conceive why he had not resolved this problem when he had nearly two months in which to select and fortify this camp. In a period of a few days a good army of 35,000 to 45,000 men should render its camp unassailable by an army twice its size, especially when it is supported by a strong fortress and a formidable river.

Tenth Observation. The battle of Leuthen is a masterpiece of movements, maneuvers, and resolution; it alone would suffice to immortalize Frederick and rank him among the greatest generals. He attacks an army stronger than his own, in position and victorious, with an army composed in part of troops who had lately been defeated, and wins a complete victory without paying for it by a loss disproportionate to the result.

All of his maneuvers in this battle have conformed to the principles of war. He did not make a flank march in front of the enemy, because the two armies did not see each other in line of battle. The Austrian army, which was aware of the approach of the King's army by the combats of Neumarkt and Borne, waited to see him take up position on the heights opposite, while Frederick, under cover of a hill and fog, and masked by his advance guard, continued his march and attacked the extreme left of the Austrian army.

Nor did Frederick violate a second principle no less sacred, that of not abandoning his line of operation. But he changed it, which is considered the most skillful maneuver taught by the art of war. In effect, an army that changes its line of operation deceives the enemy, who no longer knows which is its rear and the sensitive points by which one can threaten it. By his march Frederick abandoned the line of operation from Neumarkt and took that from Upper Silesia. The boldness and the rapidity of execution and the intrepidness of both generals and soldiers were equal to the skill of the maneuver.

Once engaged, Daun did everything that he should have done,

yet he did not succeed. Three times he attempted to refuse his left and his center by a backward wheel to the left into line; he even advanced his right to harass the line of operation from Neumarkt, which he assumed was still Frederick's line of operation. He therefore did everything that was prescribed in such circumstances. But the Prussian cavalry and the masses arrived constantly against his troops before they had time to form.

It is also true to point out that the King was marvelously helped by circumstances; all of the inferior troops, those from the empire, were on the left of the Austrian army—and the difference between troops is immense.[2]

Notes

Chapter I
Creating the Fighting Force

1. "Dix-huit notes sur l'ouvrage intitulé considérations sur l'art de la guerre," *Correspondance de Napoléon Ier,* 32 vols. (Paris: H. Plon, 1858–70), XXXI, pp. 303–4.
2. Napoleon to General Clarke, 25 October 1813, *Corres.,* XXVI, no. 20835, p. 382.
3. Napoleon to General Dejean, 26 May 1806, *Corres.,* XII, no. 10282, p. 406.
4. Napoleon to Marshal Kellermann, 4 June 1807, *Corres.,* XV, no. 12722, p. 310.
5. Napoleon to Marshal Davout, 20 July 1811, *Corres.,* XXII, no. 17935, pp. 337–38.
6. "Notes . . . sur l'art de la guerre," *Corres.,* XXXI, p. 304.
7. Napoleon to Fouché Clarke, *Corres.,* XXVI, no. 20835, p. 383.
8. "Notes sur l'art de la guerre," *Corres.,* XXXI, pp. 304–5.
9. Napoleon to Fouché, 6 August 1805, in Léon Lecestre, *Lettres inédites de Napoléon I,* 2 vols. (Paris: Plon, 1887), I, no. 85, p. 125.
10. Napoleon to Jerome, 3 April 1807, *Corres.,* XV, no. 12282, p. 16.
11. Order of the Day, 11 June 1796, *Corres.,* I, no. 615, p. 390.
12. Napoleon to the Executive Directory, 6 April 1796, *Corres.,* I, no. 121, p. 125.
13. Napoleon to Joseph, 20 August 1806, *Corres.,* XIII, no. 10672, p. 87.
14. Napoleon to Joseph, 12 August 1806, *Corres.,* XIII, no. 10635, p. 68.
15. Napoleon to Marshal Berthier, 9 March 1805, *Corres.,* X, no. 8407, pp. 207–8. In the original the fourth column referred specifically to "the conscription of the year XIII," and in the fifth, to "reserves from the years XI and XII." According to Baron de Méneval, who served as Napoleon's secretary from 1802 to 1813, these reports, which were supplied by the ministers of

war and marine, were drawn up according to Napoleon's specifications. "They were divided into columns indicating the number of the infantry and cavalry regiments, the names of the colonels, the number of men composing each battalion, squadron, and company, the Departments where they were recruited, and the number of men drafted from the Conscriptions, the places where the regiments were garrisoned, the position and strength of the depots, and the state of their troops and matériel. . . . If, during his campaigns, he fell in with isolated soldiers or small bodies of men, he could tell them at once, from a glance at their regimental number, where to go and what stages to pass under way."

The naval reports "contained the names of warships of every class, the names of their commanding officers, the composition and strength of the crews, the names of the Departments where sailors and marines were levied, the names of ships which were in docks, and particulars as to what progress had been made in their construction." Napoleon "always had a strange pleasure in receiving these reports. He used to read them through with delight." Baron Claude-François de Méneval, *Memoirs Illustrating the History of Napoleon I from 1802 to 1815*, 4 vols. (New York: D. Appleton and Company, 1894), I, pp. 370–71.

16. Napoleon to Berthier, 25 March 1803, *Corres.*, VIII, no. 6652, pp. 257–58. In the drill manuals of that day there normally were three sections—the *School of the Soldier,* which instructed the recruit in the several positions, facings, and steps of the individual soldier, the manual of arms, the different firings (by rank, by file, direct, oblique and so on), and the principles of alignment for the squad; the *School of the Company,* which prepared soldiers for the various exercises required to march, form a column, and fire; and the *School of the Battalion,* which contained those exercises and maneuvers that the battalion must master to function in battle.
17. Napoleon to General Marmont, 12 March 1804, *Corres.*, IX, no. 7616, p. 287.
18. Napoleon to Marshal Bessières, 25 May 1808, *Corres.*, XVII, no. 13984, p. 199.
19. In the context of drill a division was two platoons—which at this time were identical with companies—on line. A division therefore was a tactical formation rather than a subunit in the regiment. Colonel H. C. B. Rogers, *Napoleon's Army* (New York: Hippocrene Books, 1982), p. 62. An excellent discussion of French tactical formations during this period is found in Robert S. Quimby, *The Background of Napoleonic Warfare: The Theory of Military Tactics in Eighteenth-Century France* (New York: Columbia University Press, 1957), pp. 300–44 passim.
20. Napoleon to Bertrand, 2 March 1813, *Corres.*, XXV, no. 19643, pp. 12–13.
21. Napoleon to Marmont, 17 April 1813, *Corres.*, XXV, no. 19868, p. 201.
22. Napoleon to Joseph, 18 October 1807, *Corres.*, XVI, no. 13271, p. 101.
23. Lecestre, *Lettres inédites,* I, no. 335, p. 229. Napoleon never forgave General Pierre Antoine, Comte Dupont de l'Étang, for his capitulation at Bailén on 21 July 1808. Facing a massive uprising and cut off by Spanish forces more than twice the size of his column, Dupont made five attempts to break out before he capitulated. "Dupont has dishonored our colors," Napoleon wrote in

anger to Joseph. "What ineptitude! What baseness!" Napoleon to Joseph, 3 August 1808, *Corres.*, XVII, no. 14243, p. 428.

24. Napoleon to the Landammann of Switzerland, 18 May 1807, *New Letters of Napoleon I, Omitted from the Edition Published Under the Auspices of Napoleon III;* from the French by Lady Mary Loyd. (New York: D. Appleton and Company, 1897), p. 42. Minor liberties have been taken with Loyd's translation for the sake of greater clarity and consistency in style.
25. "33rd Bulletin of the Grande Armée," 7 December 1805, *Corres.*, XI, no. 9550, p. 464.
26. When asked on St. Helena whether Poles would be as good as French soldiers in a less rigorous climate, Napoleon responded: "Oh no, no. In other countries the French are indeed superior to them." He did acknowledge, however, that "during the rigor of winter, when the thermometer dropped to 18 degrees, it was impossible to make French soldiers remain as sentinels at their post, while the Poles did not suffer." Quoted in Lt. Col. Ernest Picard, *Préceptes et jugements de Napoléon* (Paris: Berger-Levrault, 1913), p. 254.
27. Napoleon to Jerome , 11 September 1810, *Corres.*, XXI, no. 16894, p. 102.
28. Napoleon to Clarke, 3 August 1811, *Corres.*, XXII, no. 17982, p. 368.
29. Decision, 2 November 1809, in Lt. Col. Ernest Picard and Louis Tuetey, *Unpublished Correspondence of Napoleon I,* Preserved in the War Archives, Louise Seymour Houghton, trans., 3 vols. (New York: Duffield and Company, 1913), III, p. 302.
30. Napoleon to Joseph, 12 January 1806, *Corres.*, XI, no. 9665, p. 535.
31. "Notes sur l'art de la guerre," *Corres.*, XXXI, p. 417.

Chapter II
Preparations for War

1. Napoleon to Dejean, 25 March 1807, *Corres.*, XIV, no. 12162, p. 524.
2. Napoleon to Eugene, 8 January 1806, *Corres.*, XI, no. 9660, p. 531.
3. Napoleon to Eugene, 4 November 1806, *Corres.*, XIII, no. 11172, p. 477.
4. Napoleon to Clarke, 18 August 1809, *Corres.*, XIX, no. 15678, p. 361.
5. Napoleon to Eugene, 25 March 1807, *Corres.*, XIV, no. 12174, p. 534.
6. Order of the Day, 20 March 1799, *Corres.*, V, no. 4046, p. 369.
7. Order of the Army, 12 December 1808, *Corres.*, XVIII, no. 14552, pp. 112–13.
8. To the Executive Directory, 24 April 1796, *Corres.*, I, no. 220, p. 179.
9. Napoleon to A. M. Battaglia, 10 December 1796, *Corres.*, II, no. 1257, p. 156.
10. *New Letters of Napoleon I,* trans. by Lady Mary Loyd, p. 42.
11. Napoleon to Eugene, 24 March 1806, *Corres.*, XII, no. 10015, p. 215.
12. Napoleon to Berthier, 11 November 1798, *Corres.*, V, no. 3606, p. 128.
13. Napoleon to Eugene, 1 September 1805, *Corres.*, XI, no. 9174, p. 172.
14. Ibid., p. 174.
15. Napoleon to Bertrand, 25 August 1805, *Corres.*, XI, no. 9133, pp. 136–37.

16. Napoleon to Eugene, 30 September 1805, *Corres.*, XI, no. 9300, p. 268.
17. Napoleon to Berthier, 3 March 1806, *Corres.*, XII, no. 9919, p. 127.
18. Napoleon to Bertrand, 4 March 1807, *Corres.*, XIV, no. 11929, p. 371.
19. "Observations on Affairs in Spain," 27 August 1808, *Corres.*, XVII, no. 14276, pp. 470–71.
20. Napoleon to Berthier, 3 April 1801, *Corres.*, VII, no. 5501, p. 102.
21. "Note for the War Minister," 2 August 1802, *Corres.*, VII, no. 6225, p. 546.
22. Napoleon to Baron de Saint-Aignan, 20 April 1813, *Corres.*, XXV, no. 19888, p. 215. See also "Observations on Affairs in Spain," 27 August 1808, *Corres.*, XVII, no. 14276, p. 450. Caesar François de Cassini, the greatest mapmaker of the century, started triangulation in France in 1744. After forty-five years' work he produced in 1789 the Carte Géométrique de France. R. V. Tooley, *Maps and Map-makers* (London: B. T. Batsford, 1949).
23. Napoleon to Baron de Saint-Aignan, 20 April 1813, *Corres.*, XXV, no. 19888, p. 215.
24. Napoleon to Clarke, 19 December 1809, *Corres.*, XX, no. 16075, p. 79.
25. Orders, 9 August 1809, *Corres.*, XIX, no. 15632, pp. 327–28.
26. Napoleon to Clarke, 15 November 1807, *Corres.*, XVI, no. 13360, pp. 165–66.
27. Arrêté, 15 February 1800, *Corres.*, VI, no. 4595, p. 132.
28. Napoleon to Fouché, 12 September 1805, *Corres.*, XI, no. 9202, pp. 188–89.
29. Napoleon to Clarke, 10 October 1809, *Corres.*, XIX, p. 570–71.
30. Napoleon to Berthier, 1 May 1809, *Corres.*, XVIII, no. 15148, p. 526.
31. *Corres.*, XXXI, p. 366.

Chapter III
A Military Education

1. Napoleon to Clarke, 1 October 1809, *Corres.*, XIX, no. 15889, pp. 540–42.
2. "Notes sur l'art de la guerre," *Corres.*, XXXI, p. 365.
3. "Observations sur un project d'établissement d'une école spéciale, de littérature et d'histoire au collège de France, 19 April 1807, *Corres.*, XV, no. 12416, pp. 102–10 passim.
4. Count de Las Cases, *Mémorial de Sainte Hélène, ou journal, où se trouve consigné, jour par jour, ce qu'a dit et fait Napoléon durant dix-huit mois*, 8 vols. (Paris, 1824), VII, pp. 417–18.
5. Ibid., pp. 338–39.
6. Ibid., pp. 335–36.
7. "Notes sur l'art de la guerre," *Corres.*, XXXI, pp. 347–49.
8. General G. Gourgaud, *Sainte Hélène, journal inédit*, 2 vols. (Paris, 1899), II, p. 45.
9. Las Cases, *Mémorial de Sainte Hélène*, VII, pp. 336–37.
10. "Notes sur l'art de la guerre," *Corres.*, XXXI, pp. 349–50.
11. Ibid., pp. 350–54 passim.
12. Picard, *Préceptes et jugements*, p. 363.
13. *Corres.*, XXXI, p. 354.
14. Picard, *Préceptes et jugements*, p. 418.

15. Ibid., p. 560.
16. "Notes sur l'art de la guerre," *Corres.*, XXXI, pp. 354–55.
17. Picard, *Préceptes et jugements*, pp. 560–61.
18. "Notes sur l'art de la guerre," *Corres.*, XXXI, p. 355.
19. "Précis des Guerres de Frédéric II," *Corres.*, XXXII, pp. 184–85.
20. Gourgaud, *Sainte Hélène, journal inédit*, II, p. 20.
21. Ibid., p. 32.
22. Ibid., pp. 239–40, 243.
23. Picard, *Préceptes et jugements*, p. 210.
24. "Extraits de récits de la captivité," *Corres.*, XXXII, p. 379.

Chapter IV
The Combat Arms

1. "Notes sur l'art de la guerre," *Corres.*, XXXI, p. 309.
2. "Projet d'une nouvelle organisation de l'armée," *Corres.*, XXXI, p. 438.
3. "Notes sur l'introduction à l'histoire de la guerre en Allemagne en 1756," *Corres.*, XXXI, p. 422.
4. Napoleon to Marmont, 13 October 1813, *Corres.*, XXVI, no. 20791, p. 350.
5. "Projet d'une nouvelle organisation de l'armée," *Corres.*, XXXI, pp. 444–45.
6. Napoleon to Berthier, 22 December 1803, *Corres.*, IX, no. 7415, p. 167.
7. "Projet d'une nouvelle organisation de l'armée," *Corres.*, XXXI, 453.
8. Napoleon to Joseph, 4 November 1806, *Corres.*, XIII, no. 11173, p. 479.
9. "Projet d'une nouvelle organisation de l'armée," *Corres.*, XXXI, p. 453. Napoleon's intent in this passage is clear: the proportion of cavalry to infantry in large measure depends on the terrain, and the vast plains of Poland make it ideal cavalry country.
10. "Notes sur l'art de la guerre," *Corres.*, XXXI, p. 410.
11. "Projet d'une nouvelle organisation de l'armée," *Corres.*, XXXI, p. 453.
12. "Observations sur les campagnes de 1796 et 1797," *Corres.*, XXIX, p. 338.
13. Napoleon to Joseph, 9 August 1806, *Corres.*, XIII, no. 10629, p. 63.
14. "Projet d'une nouvelle organisation de l'armée," *Corres.*, XXXI, pp. 453–54; "Notes sur l'art de la guerre," *Corres.*, XXXI, p. 324.
15. "Arrêté, 3 September 1802," *Corres.*, VIII, no. 6301, p. 22.
16. "Note Concerning the Organization of Regiments of Scouts," 9 July 1806, *Corres.*, XII, no. 10473, pp. 527–28.
17. "Projet d'une nouvelle organisation de l'armée," *Corres.*, XXXI, pp. 454–55.
18. Ibid., p. 455.
19. "Notes sur l'art de la guerre," *Corres.*, XXXI, p. 320.
20. Napoleon to Clarke, 21 November 1810, Picard and Tuetey, *Unpublished Correspondence*, III, no. 4836, p. 901.
21. "Notes sur l'art de la guerre," *Corres.*, XXXI, p. 320.
22. Ibid., pp. 320–22. *En échiquier:* "An ancient order of battle, in which the legion stood with five or more fronts upon different lines, with intermediate distances . . . somewhat similar to a chess-board." James, *New and Enlarged Dictionary in French and English* (London: T. Egerton, 1810).

23. Ibid., pp. 320–22. Napoleon here refers to the Hungarian Pandours, which had constantly harassed Frederick the Great's armies in camp and in the field.
24. Ibid., pp. 321–22.
25. Napoleon to Joseph, 20 August 1806, *Corres.*, XIII, no. 10673, p. 88.
26. "Projet d'une nouvelle organisation de l'armée," *Corres.*, XXXI, p. 456.
27. "Notes sur l'art de la guerre," *Corres.*, XXXI, pp. 322–23.
28. Napoleon to Eugene, 15 April 1806, *Corres.*, XII, no. 10104, p. 288.
29. Napoleon to Bessières, 16 April 1808, *Corres.*, XVII, no. 13751, p. 14.
30. Napoleon to Eugene, 13 March 1806, *Corres.*, XII, no. 9966, p. 183.
31. Napoleon to General Lacuée, 15 March 1807, *Corres.*, XIV, no. 12042, p. 449.
32. Napoleon to Clarke, 12 November 1811, *Corres.*, XXIII, no. 18248, p. 4.
33. "Projet d'une nouvelle organisation de l'armée," *Corres.*, XXXI, pp. 456–57. Napoleon's table of organization for cavalry in his dictations at St. Helena had changed since 1811, when he specified that the cuirassier division would contain three regiments of cuirassiers, each 900 strong, plus one regiment of lancers 800 strong, making a division of 3,500. (Napoleon to General Clarke, 25 December 1811, *Corres.*, XXIII, no. 18366, pp. 105–6.)

    After the Russian campaign the size of the regiment was smaller, and in 1813 Napoleon specified 600 men for every regiment of heavy cavalry and 100 for each regiment of light cavalry. His brigade and division organization remained essentially unchanged except when it was necessary to compress them "according to circumstances." (Napoleon to Eugene, 27 January 1813, *Corres.*, XXIV, no. 19522, pp. 463–64.)
34. Napoleon to Berthier, 22 December 1803, *Corres.*, IX, no. 7416, p. 168.
35. Napoleon to Berthier, 10 November 1804, *Corres.*, X, no. 8171, p. 48.
36. Napoleon to the minister of war, 9 January 1798, *Corres.*, III, no. 2402, p. 471.
37. Napoleon to Berthier, 1 January 1805, *Corres.*, X, no. 8251, p. 100.
38. Napoleon to General Bernadotte, 27 February 1807, *Corres.*, XIV, no. 11896, p. 346.
39. Napoleon to Eugene, 20 November 1813, *Corres.*, XXVI, no. 20929, p. 458.
40. "Notes sur l'art de la guerre," *Corres.*, XXXI, pp. 328–29.
41. Note, 30 August 1795, *Corres.*, I, no. 61, p. 85.
42. "Diplomatie . . . guerre," *Corres.*, XXX, p. 447.
43. Napoleon to the Committee of Public Safety, 25 October 1793, *Corres.*, I, no. 1, p. 11.
44. "Notes sur l'art de la guerre," *Corres.*, XXXI, p. 329.
45. Napoleon to Clarke, 15 July 1809, *Corres.*, XIX, no. 15530, p. 248.
46. Napoleon to Jerome, 12 April 1811, *Corres.*, XXII, no. 17603, p. 58.
47. "Notes sur l'art de la guerre," *Corres.*, XXXI, p. 411.
48. Napoleon to Davout, 10 May 1811, *Corres.*, XXII, no. 17708, pp. 149–50.
49. Napoleon to Clarke, 29 May 1809, *Corres.*, XIX, no. 15273, p. 58.
50. Napoleon to General Songis, 22 December 1805, *Corres.*, XI, no. 9603, p. 496.
51. Napoleon to Clarke, 18 January 1814, *Corres.*, XXVII, no. 21111, p. 51.
52. Gourgaud, *Sainte Hélène*, II, p. 460.
53. Napoleon to Berthier, 19 February 1814, *Corres.*, XXVII, no. 21303, p. 199.

54. Comte de Montholon, as quoted in Picard, *Préceptes et jugements,* p. 33.
55. *Mémoires pour servir à l'histoire de France sous Napoléon, écrits à Sainte Hélène,* 8 vols. (Paris, 1822–25), I, p. 40. This passage also appears in the various editions of Napoleon's *Maximes de guerre et pensées de Napoléon* (Paris, 5th ed., 1874), p. 43. Although not included in the *Oeuvres de Napoléon,* this passage was dictated to General Gourgaud, usually a faithful recorder of Napoleon's conversations, and the ideas are consistent with Napoleon's thoughts on the versatility of a good artillery officer.
56. "Notes sur un projet de règlement pour l'école d'artillerie et du génie," *Corres.,* VII, no. 5621, pp. 183–85.

Chapter V
Generalship and the Art of Command

1. "Notes sur les affaires d'Espagne," 30 August 1808, *Corres.,* XVII, no. 14283, p. 480.
2. Picard, *Préceptes et jugements,* pp. 116–17.
3. "Observations sur les opérations militaires: des campagnes de 1796 et 1797," *Corres.,* XXIX, p. 341.
4. Napoleon to Clarke, 11 June 1809, *Corres.,* XIX, no. 15332, p. 96.
5. "Note sur l'armée d'Italie," 19 January 1796, *Corres.,* I, no. 83, p. 104.
6. "Observations sur les . . . campagnes de 1796 et 1797," *Corres.,* XXIX, pp. 328–30.
7. "Notes sur l'art de la guerre," *Corres.,* XXXI, p. 418.
8. Napoleon to the Executive Directory, 14 May 1796, *Corres.,* I, no. 420, pp. 277–78.
9. Napoleon to Lazare Carnot, 14 May 1796, *Corres.,* I, no. 421, p. 279.
10. Napoleon to the Executive Directory, 21 June 1796, *Corres.,* I, no. 664, p. 419.
11. "Précis des Guerres de Frédéric II," *Corres.,* XXXII, pp. 182–83.
12. "Campagnes d'Italie de 1796 et 1797," *Corres.,* XXIX, p. 149.
13. Gourgaud as quoted in Picard, *Préceptes et jugements,* p. 115.
14. "Ulm-Moreau," *Corres.,* XXX, p. 412.
15. Montholon as quoted in Picard, *Préceptes et jugements,* p. 464.
16. Napoleon to Joseph, 6 June 1806, *Corres.,* XII, no. 10325, p. 442.
17. Napoleon to Eugene, 18 September 1806, *Corres.,* XIII, no. 10809, p. 208.
18. Napoleon to General Murat, 14 March 1808, *Corres.,* XVI, no. 13652, p. 418.
19. "Ulm-Moreau," *Corres.,* XXX, p. 409.
20. "Notes sur l'art de la guerre," *Corres.,* XXXI, p. 417.
21. "Notes sur la situation actuelle de l'Espagne," 5 August 1808, *Corres.,* XVII, no. 14245, p. 429.
22. Napoleon to Jerome, 2 May 1807, *Corres.,* XV, no. 12511, p. 178.
23. Napoleon to Joseph, 30 July 1806, *Corres.,* XIII, no. 10572, pp. 20–21.
24. Picard, *Préceptes et jugements,* p. 395.
25. Ibid., p. 405.
26. Ibid., pp. 362–63.

27. Ibid., p. 560.
28. Napoleon to Joseph, 3 August 1808, *Corres.*, XVII, no. 14243, p. 428. The verb tense has been changed for the sake of consistency. Napoleon also advised that "Ney is a brave man, zealous, and all heart. If you get used to him he would be good to command [your] army."
29. "Campagne de 1815," *Corres.*, XXXI, p. 188.
30. Picard, *Préceptes et jugements*, p. 524.
31. Ibid., p. 499.
32. Napoleon to Berthier, 10 April 1806, *Corres.*, XII, no. 10074, p. 270.
33. Napoleon to General Mortier, 29 October 1806, *Corres.*, XIII, no. 11325, p. 588.
34. Napoleon to Eugene, 21 August 1806, *Corres.*, XIII, no. 10681, p. 96.
35. Napoleon to Joseph, 10 November 1808, *Corres.*, XVIII, no. 14460, p. 51.
36. Napoleon to Joseph, 6 June 1806, *Corres.*, XII, no. 10325, p. 440.
37. "Campagnes d'Egypte et de Syrie," *Corres.*, XXX, p. 130.
38. "Campagnes d'Italie," *Corres.*, XXIX, p. 108.
39. "Notes sur l'art de la guerre," *Corres.*, XXXI, p. 380.
40. Napoleon to the Executive Directory, 6 May 1796, *Corres.*, I, no. 338, p. 238.
41. "Campagnes d'Italie," *Corres.*, XXIX, pp. 107–8.
42. Picard, *Préceptes et jugements*, p. 383.
43. "Notes-Moreau," *Corres.*, XXX, p. 496.
44. Picard, *Préceptes et jugements*, p. 493.
45. Napoleon to Bessières, 20 November 1809, in Picard, *Préceptes et jugements*, pp. 420–21.
46. "Campagne de 1815," *Corres.*, XXXI, p. 207.
47. "Précis des guerres du maréchal de Turenne," *Corres.*, XXXII, p. 100.
48. Napoleon to the minister of foreign relations, 1 October 1797, *Corres.*, III, no. 2272, p. 357.
49. Picard, *Préceptes et jugements*, pp. 114–15.
50. Napoleon to Bertrand, 6 June 1813, *Corres.*, XXV, no. 20090, p. 363.
51. Las Cases, *Memoirs and Conversations*, pp. 250–51.
52. Napoleon to Berthier, 9 April 1810, *Corres.*, XX, no. 16372, p. 284.
53. Napoleon to Eugene, 30 April 1809, *Corres.*, XVIII, no. 15144, p. 525.
54. Napoleon to Joseph, 26 June 1806, *Corres.*, XII, no. 10416, p. 489.
55. Napoleon to Joseph, 4 March 1809, *Corres.*, XVIII, no. 14846, p. 308.
56. Napoleon to Joseph, 26 June 1806, *Corres.*, XII, no. 10416, pp. 489–90.
57. Napoleon to Joseph, 20 March 1806, *Corres.*, XII, no. 9997, p. 204.
58. Napoleon to Joubert, 17 February 1797, *Corres.*, II, no. 1501, p. 337.
59. Napoleon to Bessières, 20 November 1809, in Picard, *Préceptes et jugements*, p. 337.
60. Napoleon to Clarke, 16 May 1811, *Corres.*, XXII, no. 17727, p. 160.
61. Napoleon to Berthier, 29 March 1811, *Corres.*, XXI, no. 17529, p. 523.
62. Napoleon to Berthier, 9 July 1812, *Corres.*, XXIV, no. 18936, pp. 40–41.
63. Napoleon to Citizen Letourneur, 6 May 1796, *Corres.*, I, no. 339, pp. 238–39.
64. Napoleon to Rear Admiral ver Huell, 21 May 1804, *Corres.*, IX, no. 7766, pp. 368–69.

CHAPTER VI
ARMY ORGANIZATION

1. Napoleon to Lacuée, 2 June 1805, *Corres.*, X, no. 8829, p. 472.
2. Napoleon to the King of Holland, 5 August 1806, *Corres.*, XIII, no. 10601, p. 39.
3. "Observations sur les . . . campagnes de 1796 et 1797, *Corres.*, XXIX, p. 342.
4. Picard, *Préceptes et jugements*, pp. 175–76.
5. Ibid., p. 176.
6. "Project d'une nouvelle organisation de l'armée," *Corres.*, XXXI, pp. 458–59. Napoleon to Berthier, 25 January 1800, *Corres.*, XI, no. 4552, p. 107. It is interesting that Napoleon would not organize an army of 80,000 into permanent corps, for in the next major conflict—the American Civil War—most armies in the field quickly adapted the corps organization, or at least an ad hoc arrangement in which several divisions were coordinated by "wing commanders." After the first year of campaigning, most Union and Confederate armies of any size were organized by corps. In the Confederate army a corps commander had the rank of lieutenant general, as Napoleon specified for anyone commanding or even coordinating two or more divisions. In the Union army, however, it was most often a major general and occasionally even a brigadier.

   No doubt this reflected Napoleon's experience in the Italian campaigns, where his army numbered about 60,000 men divided into divisions, each of 3,000 to 9,000 men. Such an arrangement worked for Napoleon in 1796–97 because of the mountainous terrain, the experience of his subordinate commanders, and his own ability to outmaneuver his enemy who were similarly dispersed—and yet concentrate before battle.
7. Napoleon to Berthier, 25 January 1800, *Corres.*, VI, no. 4552, p. 107.
8. "Plan de campagne pour l'armée du Rhin," 22 March 1800, *Corres.*, VI, no. 4694, p. 201.
9. Napoleon to Berthier, 29 August 1805, *Corres.*, XI, no. 9158, p. 159.
10. Napoleon to Eugene, 7 June 1809, *Corres.*, XIX, no. 15310, p. 81.
11. Napoleon to Marmont, 18 February 1812, *Corres.*, XXIII, no. 18503, p. 234.

CHAPTER VII
STRATEGY

1. Published in Capt. J. Colin, *L'éducation militaire de Napoléon* (Paris: Librairie Militaire, R. Chapelot et Cie, 1901), pp. 443–47. Colin makes a convincing case for attributing the authorship to Napoleon (p. 295). The document was carried by Augustin Robespierre to the Committee of Public Safety in June 1794. Two years later Napoleon was given the opportunity to execute it.
2. "Note," *Corres.*, III, no. 2411, pp. 484–85.
3. "Order," *Corres.*, V, no. 3439, p. 41.
4. Napoleon to General Moreau, 22 March 1800, *Corres.*, VI, no. 4695, pp. 203–4.

5. Napoleon to Masséna, 9 April 1800, *Corres.*, VI, no. 4711, pp. 214–16.
6. *Corres.*, XXX, pp. 399–400.
7. Berthier to General Gouvion St. Cyr, 2 September 1805, *Corres.*, XI, no. 9176, pp. 173–75.
8. Napoleon to Joseph, 31 December 1805, *Corres.*, XI, no. 9633, p. 519.
9. Napoleon to Joseph, 12 January 1806, *Corres.*, XI, no. 9665, pp. 534–36.
10. Napoleon to Joseph, 19 January 1806, *Corres.*, XI, no. 9685, pp. 546–47.
11. Napoleon to Joseph, 7 February 1808, *Corres.*, XVI, no. 13537, pp. 313–14.
12. On 14 July 1808, French forces under Marshal Bessières attacked and defeated local patriot armies of Castile and Galicia, encouraging Napoleon to adjust his strategic plan for the conquest of Spain.
13. "Notes on the Actual Position of the Army in Spain," 21 July 1808, *Corres.*, XVII, no. 14223, pp. 409–13. On 5 July 1807, about 4,500 British troops in three columns commanded by Lieutenant General John Whitelocke attempted to seize Buenos Aires at a cost of nearly 3,000 casualties.
14. Ibid., pp. 409–13.

Chapter VIII
Fortification

1. Napoleon to Dejean, 27 June 1806, *Corres.*, XII, no. 10419, p. 492.
2. "Notes sur l'art de la guerre," *Corres.*, XXXI, p. 420.
3. "Notes sur l'art de la guerre," *Corres.*, XXXI, pp. 335–36.
4. Ibid., pp. 335–36. In 1793 General Charles-François du Périer Dumouriez, then commanding the *Armée du Nord,* had deserted to the Austrians in an unsuccessful effort to reestablish the monarch.
5. Napoleon to Dejean, 3 September 1806, *Corres.*, XIII, no. 10726, p. 131.
6. Ibid., pp. 131–34.

Chapter IX
The Army in the Field

1. Napoleon to Eugene, 20 June 1809, *Corres.*, XIX, no. 15373, p. 140.
2. Napoleon to Joseph, 12 January 1806, *Corres.*, XI, no. 9665, p. 535.
3. Napoleon to Joseph, 24 September 1808, *Corres.*, XVII, no. 14347, p. 528.
4. Order of the Day, 3 October 1806, quoted in Pierron, *Stratégie et grande tactique d'après l'expérience des dernières guerres,* 4 vols. (Paris: Berger-Levrault et Cie, 1896), I, pp. 480–81.
5. Order of the Day, 12 May 1813, ibid.
6. Order of the Day, 3 October 1806, ibid., p. 479.
7. "Notes sur l'art de la guerre, *Corres.*, XXXI, pp. 355–60. Napoleon here refers to himself in the second person. It has been changed to the first person for the sake of consistency.
8. "Instructions dictated by the Emperor on the administrative services of the Grande Armée," *Corres.*, XXIII, no. 18589, pp. 321–23.

9. Napoleon to Berthier, 16 June 1812, *Corres.*, XXIII, no. 18812, pp. 504–5.
10. Napoleon to Berthier, 2 July 1812, *Corres.*, XXIV, no. 18888, p. 9.
11. Napoleon to Eugene, 22 September 1805, *Corres.*, XI, no. 9258, pp. 240–41.
12. Napoleon to A. M. Petiet, Intendant General of the Army, 24 October, 1805, *Corres.*, XI, no. 9425, p. 345.
13. Napoleon to Berthier, 29 May 1810, *Corres.*, XX, no. 16521, p. 388.
14. Napoleon to Daru, Intendant General of the Army, 27 March 1808, *Corres.*, XVI, no. 13693, pp. 447–48.
15. Napoleon to Berthier, 10 April 1809, *Corres.*, XVIII, no. 15043, pp. 456–57.
16. Gourgaud, II, p. 337, quoted in Picard, *Precéptes et jugements*, p. 71.
17. Napoleon to Berthier, 27 May 1813, quoted in ibid., p. 70.
18. Napoleon to Berthier, 23 September 1812, *Corres.*, XXIV, no. 19220, p. 227.
19. "Projet d'organisation de l'armée," *Corres.*, XXXI, pp. 449–52.
20. "Instructions dictées par l'Empéreur sur les services administratifs de la Grande Armée," 16 March 1812, *Corres.*, XXIII, no. 18589, p. 323.
21. Napoleon to Berthier, 16 June 1796, *Corres.*, I, no. 648, p. 408.
22. Pierron, *Stratégie et grande tactique,* I, 470–71.
23. Napoleon to Bessières, 16 April 1808, *Corres.*, XVII, no. 13751, pp. 14–15.
24. Napoleon to Clarke, 8 December 1806, *Corres., XIV,* no. 11412, p. 47.
25. Napoleon to General Lemarois, 3 July 1813, *Corres.*, XXV, no. 20218, p. 453.
26. Napoleon to Soult, 8 October 1803, *Corres.*, IX, no. 7180, pp. 32–33.
27. "Note for the intendant general, 8 December 1806," *Corres.*, XIV, no. 11409, p. 44.
28. Order of the Day, 26 September 1796, quoted in Pierron, *Stratégie et grande tactique,* II, pp. 727–28.
29. Napoleon to Clarke, 24 January 1809, *Corres.*, XVIII, no. 14736, p. 240.
30. *Note pour l'intendant général,* 21 December 1806, *Corres.*, XIV, no. 11508, pp. 110–11. Napoleon uses the term *ambulance,* which probably referred to the personnel and matériel of the medical service rather than to a specific vehicle that carried the wounded. According to *Scott's Military Dictionary* (1860), "in the French army, an Ambulance of infantry is composed of five wagons containing cases of instruments for amputating and trepanning, bandages for divers fractures, utensils of all kinds, medicines, and 8,900 dressings," pp. 22–23. What today is known as an ambulance was then called an ambulance cart.
31. Berthier, by order of Napoleon, to Daru, 21 December 1806, *Corres.*, XIV, no. 11507, p. 110.
32. Order of the Day, 14 May 1809, *Corres.*, XIX, no. 15205, p. 2.
33. Army Order, 22 June 1812, *Corres.*, XXIII, no. 18856, pp. 529–31. Similar provost's commissions and mobile columns of roughly the same size, but different nationalities, were ordered formed at Koenigsberg, Varsovie, Posen, Danzig, Marienwerder, and Berlin.
34. Ibid., pp. 529–31.
35. Napoleon to Berthier, 14 June 1812, *Corres.*, XXIII, no. 18791, p. 490.
36. Napoleon to General Junot, 28 January 1808, quoted from *New Letters of Napoleon I*, pp. 66–67.
37. Napoleon to Joseph, 2 March 1806, *Corres.*, XII, no. 9911, p. 121.
38. Napoleon to Joseph, 17 August, 1806, *Corres.*, XIII, no. 10657, p. 78.

39. Napoleon to Clarke, Minister of War, 24 January 1813, in *New Letters of Napoleon I,* p. 267.
40. Napoleon to Joseph, 20 March 1806, *Corres.,* XII, no. 9997, p. 204.
41. Napoleon to Joseph, 31 March 1806, *Corres.,* XII, no. 10042, p. 249.
42. Napoleon to Junot, 28 January 1808, *New Letters of Napoleon I,* p. 66.
43. Napoleon to Guillaume Brune, 4 November, 1800, *Corres.,* VI, no. 5159, p. 496.
44. Napoleon to Charles-François Lebrun, 18 March 1811, *New Letters of Napoleon I,* p. 229.
45. Napoleon to Junot, 11 April 1806, *Dernières lettres inédites de Napoléon Ier,* I, no. 398, p. 190.
46. Napoleon to Murat, 29 April, 1808, *New Letters of Napoleon I,* p. 83.
47. "Notes sur l'art de la guerre," *Corres.,* XXXI, p. 365.

Chapter X
The Operational Art

1. "Military Maxims of Napoleon," Major Thomas R. Phillips, ed., *Roots of Strategy* (Harrisburg, Pennsylvania: Military Service Publishing Company, 1941), pp. 407–41 passim. This is the best, and certainly the most readable, of the several translations I have consulted.
2. Napoleon to Berthier, 2 October, 1804, *Corres.,* X, no. 8075, p. 5.
3. Napoleon to the King of Naples, *Corres.,* XIII, no. 10810, p. 210.
4. Napoleon to the Grand Duke of Berg, *Corres.,* no. 13652, XVI, p. 418.
5. Napoleon to Joseph, 24 September 1808, *Corres.,* XVII, no. 14347, p. 528.
6. Napoleon to Alexander, Prince of Neuchâtel, 8 September 1808, *Corres.,* XVII, no. 14307, p. 502.
7. Pierre-Louis, Count Roederer, *Autour de Bonaparte,* edited by Maurice Vitrac (Paris: H. Daragon, 1909), p. 4, as quoted in J. Christopher Herold, *The Mind of Napoleon* (New York: Columbia University Press, 1955), p. 230.
8. "Précis des événements militaires arrivés pendant les six premiers mois de 1799," *Corres.,* XXX, pp. 262–63.
9. *Corres.,* III, no. 1976, p. 163.
10. *Corres.,* XXXI, p. 417.
11. "Official After-Action Report of the Battle of Austerlitz," 28 March 1806, *Corres.,* XII, no. 10032, pp. 230–31.
12. Napoleon to the King of Naples, *Corres.,* XII, no. 10467, p. 524.
13. Berthier to General Saint-Cyr, 2 September 1805, *Corres.,* XI, no. 9176, pp. 173–75 passim.
14. "Note for the King of Spain [Joseph]," *Corres.,* XVII, no. 14343, pp. 523–26.
15. *Corres.,* XIX, no. 15379, pp. 133–34.
16. "Campagnes d'Egypte et de Syrie," *Corres.,* XXX, p. 10.
17. Ibid., pp. 9–10.
18. Napoleon to Marmont, 18 February 1812, *Corres.,* XXIII, no. 18503, p. 234.
19. Picard, *Préceptes et jugements,* pp. 124, 125.

Appendix
Critical Analysis: The Wars of Frederick the Great

1. Although Napoleon here uses the word *corps,* he does not refer specifically to an army corps as it is understood today or even as he conceived and organized it in 1800. A corps in Frederick's day meant "any body of forces, destined to act together under one commander." See the definition of *corps* in Charles James, *New and Enlarged Military Dictionary, in French and English, in Which Are Explained the Principal Terms,* 3rd ed., 2 vols. (London: T. Egerton, 1810).
2. "Précis des Guerres de Frédéric II," *Corres.*, XXXII, pp. 161–85 passim.

Bibliography

Primary

Correspondance de Napoléon Ier. 32 vols. Paris: H. Plon, 1858–70; reprinted, New York: AMS Press, 1974.

Lanza, Colonel Conrad H., trans., *The Jena Campaign Source Book.* Fort Leavenworth, Kansas: The U.S. General Service Schools Press, 1922.

Lecestre, Léon, *Lettres inédites de Napoléon Ier.* 2 vols. Paris: Plon, 1887.

Maximes de guerre et pensées de Napoléon. 5th ed. Paris, 1874.

Memoirs of the History of France During the Reign of Napoleon, Dictated by the Emperor at Saint Helena to the Generals Who Shared His Captivity. 7 vols. London: Henry Colburn, 1823.

New Letters of Napoleon I, Omitted from the Edition Published Under the Auspices of Napoleon III. From the French by Lady Mary Loyd. New York: D. Appleton and Company, 1897.

"Notes sur l'artillerie dictée par Napoléon à Sainte-Hélène à Baron Gourgaud." *Revue d'Artillerie,* June 1897.

Phillips, Major Thomas R., ed., *Roots of Strategy.* Harrisburg, Pennsylvania: Military Service Publishing Company, 1941. Contains the best translations of Napoleon's Principles of War.

Picard, Lt. Col. Ernest. *Préceptes et jugements de Napoléon.* Paris: Berger-Levrault, 1913; reprinted, New York: AMS Press, 1974.

Picard, Lt. Col. Ernest, and Louis Tuetey; publishers. Translated by Louise Seymour Houghton. *Unpublished Correspondence of Napoleon I,* Preserved in the War Archives. 3 vols. New York: Duffield and Company, 1913.

SECONDARY

Clausewitz, Carl von. *The Campaign of 1812 in Russia.* Westport, Connecticut: Greenwood Press, 1977.

———. *On War.* Edited and translated by Michael Howard and Peter Paret. Princeton: University Press, 1976.

Colin, Capt. J. *L'éducation militaire de Napoléon.* Paris: Librairie Militaire, R. Chapelot et Cie, 1901.

Delbruck, Hans. *History of the Art of War Within the Framework of Political History.* Translated by Walter J. Renfroe, Jr. 4 vols. Westport, Connecticut: Greenwood Press, 1985.

Dernières lettres inédites de Napoléon Ier. Collationnées sur les textes et publiées par Léonce de Brotonne. Paris: H. Champion, 1903.

Elting, John R. *Swords Around the Throne: Napoleon's Grande Armée.* New York: The Free Press, 1988.

Fuller, Gen. J. F. C. *Training Soldiers for War.* London: Hugh Rees, 1914.

Gourgaud, General Gaspard. *Sainte Hélène, journal inédit, de 1815 à 1818.* 2 vols. Paris: 1899.

Guibert, Count de. *Defense du système de guerre moderne.* 2 vols. Neuchâtel, 1779.

Heinl, Col. Robert D., Jr. *Dictionary of Military and Naval Quotations.* Annapolis, Maryland: United States Naval Institute, 1966.

Henderson, Col. G. F. R. *Stonewall Jackson and the American Civil War.* Secaucus, New Jersey: The Blue and Grey Press, n.d.

Herold, J. Christopher. *The Mind of Napoleon.* New York: Columbia University Press, 1955.

Horne, Alistair. *How Far from Austerlitz? Napoleon, 1705–1815.* London: Macmillan, 1966.

Jähns, Max. *Geschichte der Kriegswissenschaften vornehmlich in Deutschland. III. Das 18. Jahrhundert seit dem Auftreten Friedrichs des Grossen, 1740–1800;* reprinted, New York: Johnson Reprint Corporation, 1966.

James, Charles. *New and Enlarged Military Dictionary, in French and English, in Which Are Explained the Principal Terms, with Appropriate Illustrations, of All the Sciences That Are More or Less Necessary for an Officer and Engineer,* 3rd ed. 2 vols. London: T. Egerton, 1810.

Kircheisen, F. M. *Napoleon.* London: Gerald Gowe, 1921.

Knotel, Herbert, Jr., and Herbert Sieg. *Uniforms of the World: A Compendium of Army, Navy, and Air Force Uniforms, 1700–1937.* New York: Bookthrift, 1980.

Lachouque, Henry. *Napoleon's Battles: A History of His Campaigns.* Translated by Roy Monkcom. New York: E. P. Dutton, 1967.

Las Cases, Count de. *Mémorial de Sainte Hélène, ou journal où se trouve consigné, jour par jour, ce qu'a dit et fait Napoléon durant dix-huit mois.* 8 vols. Paris, 1824.

May, Major E. S. *Guns and Cavalry: Their Performances in the Past and Their Prospects in the Future.* London: Sampson Low, Marston and Company, 1896.

Méneval, Baron Claude-François de. *Memoirs Illustrating the History of Napoleon I from 1802 to 1815*. 4 vols. New York: D. Appleton and Company, 1894.

Petre, F. Loraine. *Napoleon's Conquest of Prussia—1806*. London: John Lane Company, 1907.

Pierron, Gen. *Stratégie et grande tactique d'après l'expérience des dernières guerres*. 4 vols. Paris: Berger-Levrault et Cie, 1896.

Quimby, Robert S. *The Background of Napoleonic Warfare: The Theory of Military Tactics in Eighteenth-Century France*. New York: Columbia University Press, 1957.

Rogers, Col. H. C. B. *Napoleon's Army*. New York: Hippocrene Books, 1982.

Scott, Colonel H. L. *Military Dictionary: Comprising Technical Definitions*. Reprinted, New York: Greenwood Press, 1968.

Shafritz, Jay M., et al. *The Facts on File Dictionary of Military Science*. New York: Facts on File, 1989.

Tooley, R. V. *Maps and Map-makers*. London: B. T. Batsford, 1949.

U.S. Army Headquarters, Department of the Army, U.S. Army, FM *100-5, Operations*, 1 July 1976.

———. FM *100-5, Operations*, 5 May 1986.

———. FM *100-5, Operations*, June 1993.

U.S. War Department. *The War of the Rebellion. A Compilation of the Official Records of the Union and Confederate Armies*. Washington, 1880–1901. Series I, Volume XI.

Index

9 780684 872711